EVERYBODY'S
GUITAR TABLATURE METHOD

A STEP-BY-STEP APPROACH

Philip Groeber, David Hoge, Rey Sanchez

with CD

CONTENTS

Note: The pieces in this book are composed by the authors unless otherwise indicated.

Production: Frank and Gail Hackinson
Production Coordinator: Philip Groeber
Cover Design: Terpstra Design, San Francisco
Pilot Editor: Jay Hicks

Photography: Lynn Ivory, Master Photographer, Tallahassee
Engraving: Tempo Music Press, Inc.
Printer: Tempo Music Press, Inc.

THE
F·J·H
MUSIC
COMPANY
I N C.
Frank J. Hackinson

ISBN-13: 978-156939-934-7

TYPES OF GUITARS

There are three basic types of guitars:
 acoustic (steel string), *electric* (steel string), and *classical* (nylon string).
This book may be used with *any* type of guitar.

Acoustic

nut —
tuning pegs
neck (fingerboard)
pick guard
bridge

Electric

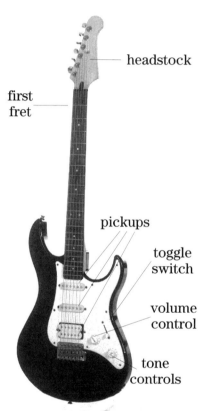

first fret
headstock
pickups
toggle switch
volume control
tone controls

Classical

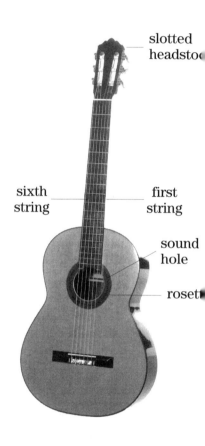

slotted headstock
sixth string
first string
sound hole
rosette
first string

The acoustic guitar has steel strings and a bright, ringing tone. Both pick-style and finger-style playing are common on the acoustic guitar.

The electric guitar is used for a wide range of musical styles. Pick-style is more common, but finger-style playing is also used. When practicing on the electric guitar, it is best to use an amplifier.

The classical guitar has nylon strings, which are easier to press down than the steel strings found on an acoustic guitar. Finger-style playing is most common.

IMPORTANT

When selecting a guitar, make sure that the instrument:
* is easy to play (easy to press the strings down);
* has a good, quality sound; and
* will stay in tune once the strings are stretched out.

HOLDING THE GUITAR

Sitting

The guitar should rest comfortably on your lap. The right leg may be crossed over the left leg for added support.

Standing

A guitar strap is used to hold the guitar in correct playing position. A strap may also be used in the sitting position.

Classical position

The left leg is raised by a footstand, which places the guitar in a very secure position.

The Left Hand

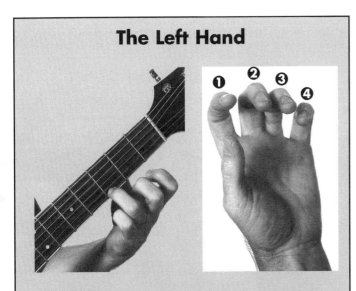

- The left-hand fingers are numbered 1, 2, 3, 4 as shown.
- Press with the fingertip directly *behind* the fret. Use just enough pressure to produce a clear sound. For best results, the left-hand fingernails should be kept short.
- The thumb should touch lightly on the back of the guitar neck opposite the fingertips. It remains in a natural position. The palm does not touch the back of the neck.

The Right Hand

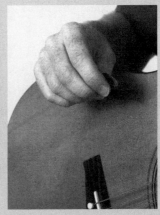

- The **pick** (flat-pick or plectrum) is used to strum the strings.
- Some students may choose to use the right-hand thumb and fingers instead of a pick.
- If using a pick, start with a teardrop shape of medium thickness.
- Hold the pick in a relaxed, secure way.
- The strings may be sounded by using **downstrokes** (◼) or **upstrokes** (v) with the guitar pick.

3

MUSIC FUNDAMENTALS

THE STAFF

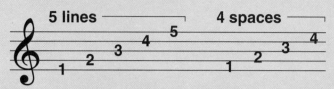

Music is written on the **staff**, which has five lines and four spaces.

THE TREBLE CLEF

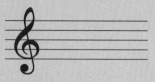

The **treble** (or **G**) **clef** is placed at the beginning (left side) of each staff of guitar music.

LINE NOTES

Each **line** has a letter name:

Every **G**uitar **B**eginner **D**oes **F**ine

SPACE NOTES

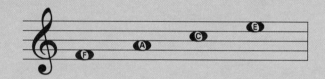

Each **space** has a letter name:

F A C E

PITCH

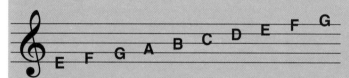

Pitch is the highness or lowness of a music tone. The higher the pitch, the higher a note is placed on the staff. The lower the pitch, the lower a note is placed on the staff. The names of notes come from the music alphabet A–G.

NOTE VALUES

o	whole note	= 4 beats
♩.	dotted half note	= 3 beats
♩	half note	= 2 beats
♩	quarter note	= 1 beat
♪	eighth note	= ½ beat

Note values (o ♩. ♩ ♩ ♪) indicate the duration of each pitch. Each musical note indicates the pitch to be played *and* how long to let the tone sound.

BAR LINES AND MEASURES

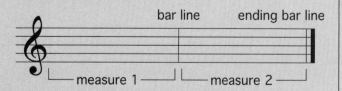

Bar lines divide the staff into equal parts called **measures**. An **ending bar line** is used to show the end of a piece of music.

THE TIME SIGNATURE

The $\frac{4}{4}$ (four-four) **time signature** tells us:

4 = four beats per measure
4 = the quarter note (♩) gets one beat

Count: 1   2   3   4

TUNING THE GUITAR

It is very important that your guitar be tuned correctly each time you practice.

1. Electronic tuner

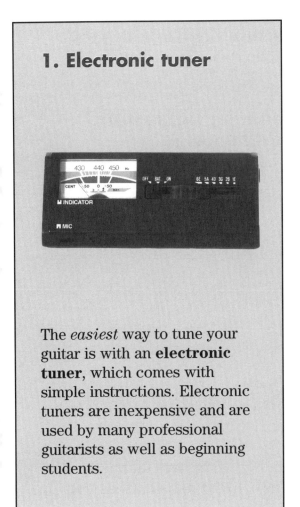

The *easiest* way to tune your guitar is with an **electronic tuner**, which comes with simple instructions. Electronic tuners are inexpensive and are used by many professional guitarists as well as beginning students.

2. Piano keyboard

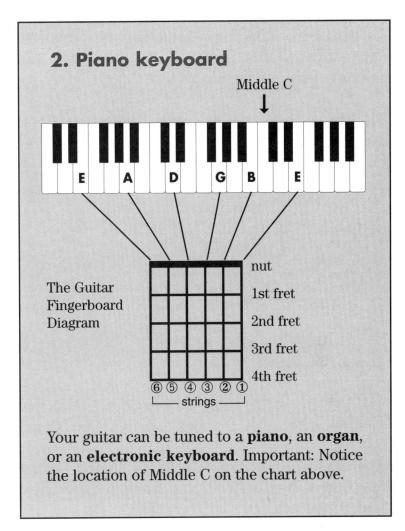

Your guitar can be tuned to a **piano**, an **organ**, or an **electronic keyboard**. Important: Notice the location of Middle C on the chart above.

3. Tuning the guitar to itself (relative tuning)

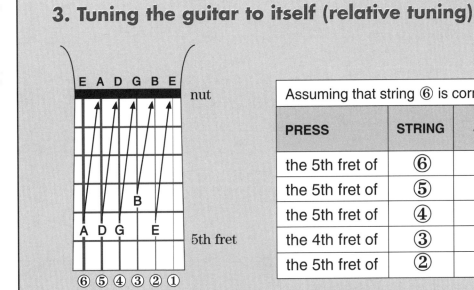

Assuming that string ⑥ is correctly tuned to E:			
PRESS	**STRING**	**TO GET THE PITCH**	**TO TUNE OPEN STRING**
the 5th fret of	⑥	**A**	⑤
the 5th fret of	⑤	**D**	④
the 5th fret of	④	**G**	③
the 4th fret of	③	**B**	②
the 5th fret of	②	**E**	①

CD TRACK

(1)   Introduction and tuning notes: E B G D A E

48

5

UNDERSTANDING TABLATURE

About Tablature

Tablature (or TAB) is often used in the notation of guitar music. This centuries old system uses six horizontal lines to represent the guitar strings, and numbers to indicate frets. Interest in tablature greatly increased around 1950, due to the sudden popularity of the guitar in popular music.

Modern guitarists need to understand standard music notation (the five-line staff), and tablature. Each notational style shows certain elements of the music:

Standard Notation
pitch (page 4)
note values (page 4)
dynamics (page 12)
articulations (page 99)

Tablature
fret number
string number
note location over the entire fretboard

Tablature Tips

Use TAB to quickly visualize if notes are on consecutive frets, on the same string, on adjacent strings, or more than two strings apart.

The fret number in the tablature will not always match the left-hand finger number that may appear next to the notehead. Associate the numbers next to the noteheads as left-hand finger numbers, NOT fret numbers.

Most of the notes on the guitar can be played in two, usually three or more different places. Tablature will show you exactly where the note to be played is located.

How to Use Tablature

In the following example of *Ode to Joy*, you would begin by playing the open first string twice, followed by the first string played at the first fret, the first string at the third fret. When the numbers are on the second line from the top, you would play on the second string.

The complete version of *Ode to Joy* is introduced on page 22.

More tablature symbols covered in this book:

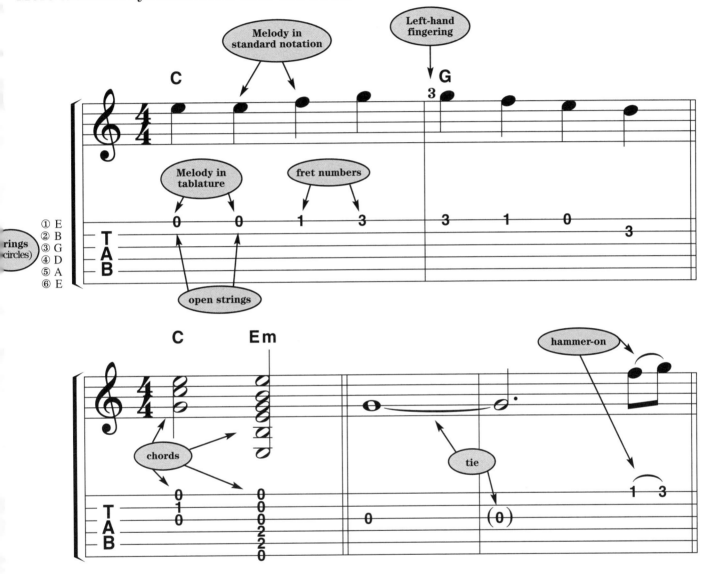

Advantages of Using Tablature

Tablature is very helpful for beginners to begin learning familiar melodies.

The guitar is one of the few instruments that can play one particular note (pitch) in several places. The use of tablature makes it exactly clear where the note is intended to be played.

Guitar tablature is the international language of rock guitarists on the internet.

NOTES ON THE FIRST STRING

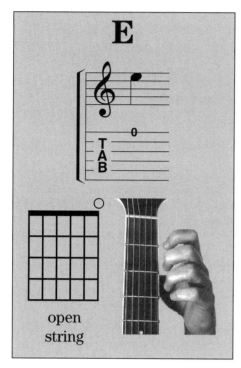

E

open string

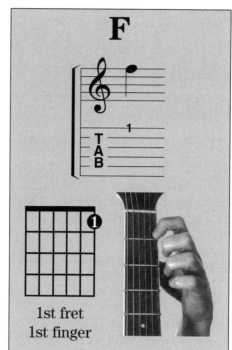

F

1st fret
1st finger

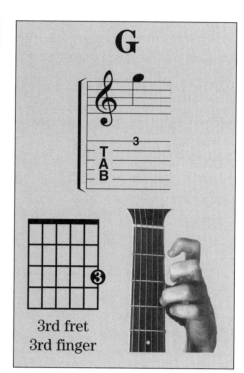

G

3rd fret
3rd finger

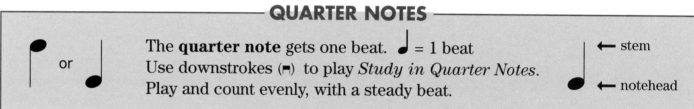

QUARTER NOTES

The **quarter note** gets one beat. ♩ = 1 beat
Use downstrokes (⊓) to play *Study in Quarter Notes*.
Play and count evenly, with a steady beat.

← stem

← notehead

The gray symbols (**E**, **F**, etc.) indicate chords to be played by the teacher.
Numbers next to the noteheads (**0**, **1**, **2**, **3**, **4**) indicate left-hand fingering.

Study in Quarter Notes

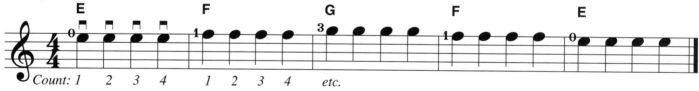

Count: 1 2 3 4   1 2 3 4   etc.

Woodstock ②

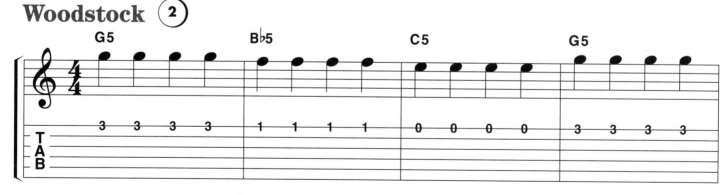

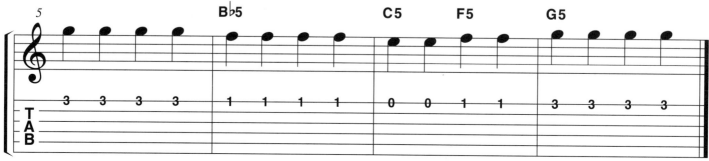

8

G

The **half note** gets two beats. ♩ = 2 beats
Be sure to let the half note ring for two full beats.

Study in Half Notes

Count: 1 – 2   3 – 4   etc.

③ The Sounds of Jazz

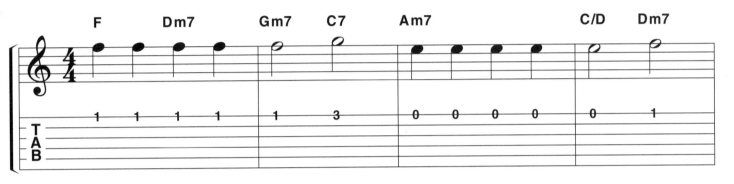

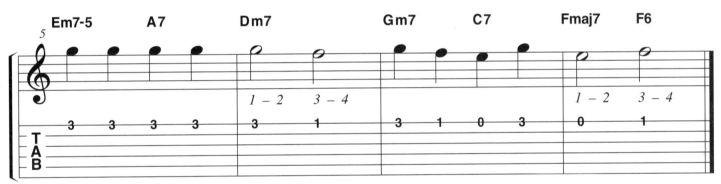

④ Summer of '59

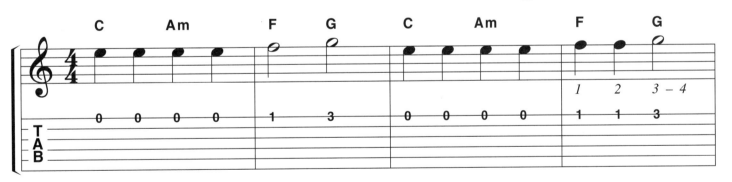

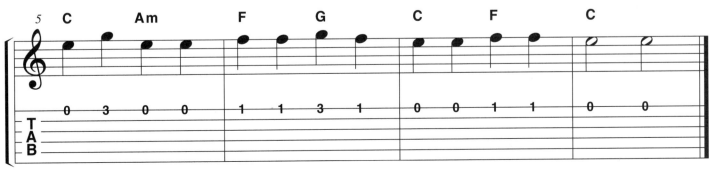

NOTES ON THE SECOND STRING

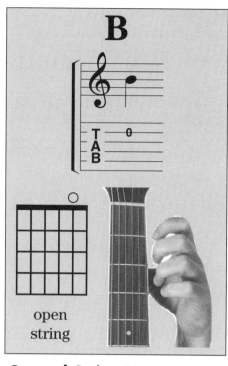

B

open string

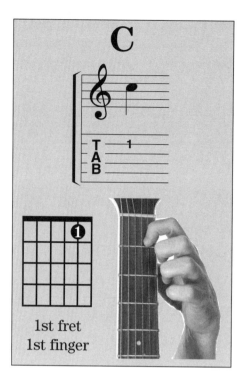

C

1st fret
1st finger

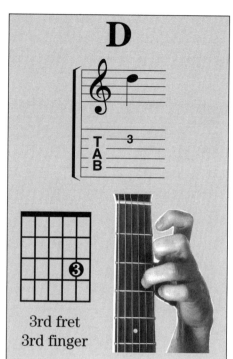

D

3rd fret
3rd finger

Second String Warm-up

Count: 1 – 2 3 4

Flamenco Fire ⑤

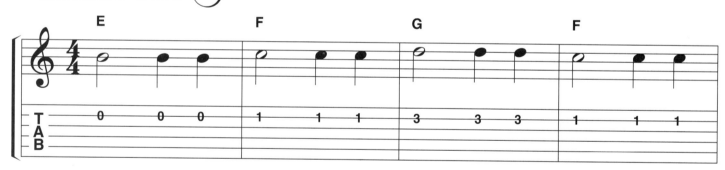

Notice that the fingering is the same for the notes you have learned on the first and second strings. Play these notes while saying the note names aloud.

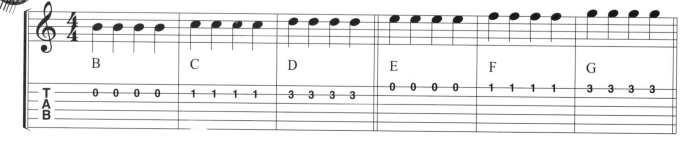

G10

WHOLE NOTES

𝐨 The whole note gets four beats. 𝐨 = 4 beats
Four even counts must take place before you play the next note.
Count "**1-2-3-4**" for each whole note. **Always keep an even, steady beat**.

Study in Whole Notes

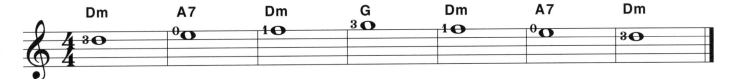

6 **Rock Legend**

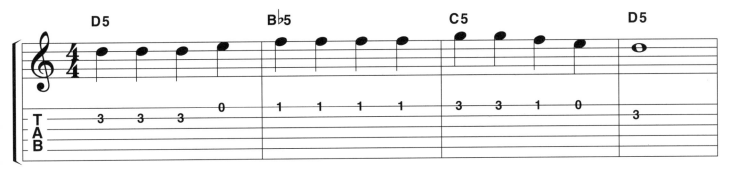

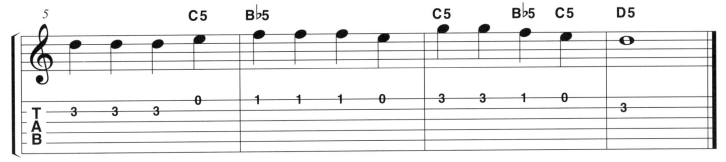

7 **Lute Melody**

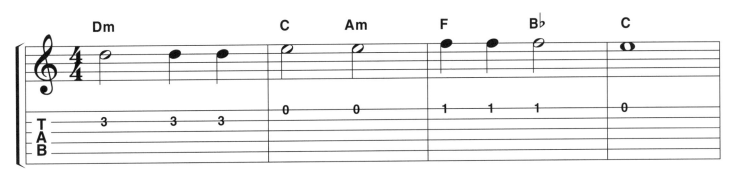

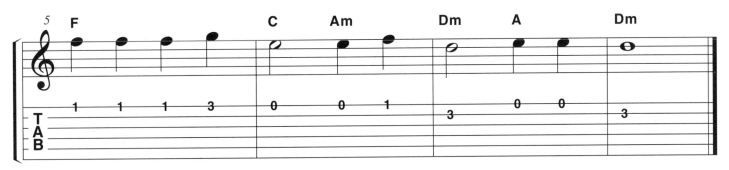

11

DYNAMICS

Dynamics are symbols and words that indicate how loud or soft to play.
The following symbols are used in this book:

p = *piano* (soft)   *mf* = *mezzo forte* (medium loud)   *f* = *forte* (loud)

If the music has no dynamic level indicated, play *mf* (medium loud).

Jingle Bells (8)

J. Pierpont

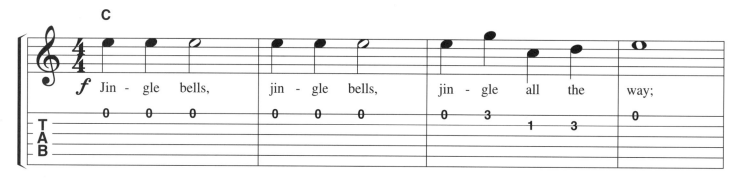

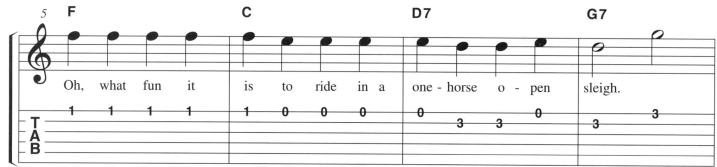

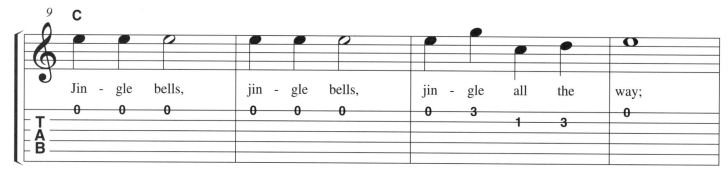

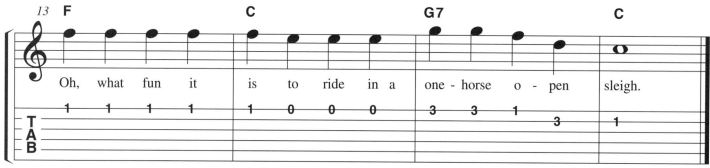

Practice any difficult sections separately from the rest of the song. Begin at a slow tempo; then gradually increase the speed. Remember that each challenge presents an opportunity for you to become a better guitarist.

(9) American Folk Song Medley

Traditional

*A double bar line indicates the end of a section of music.

Allow each note to sound as long as possible. This technique, called legato, will help you to play smoothly. Looking ahead to the next note can also help you to play legato.

Caribbean Paradise

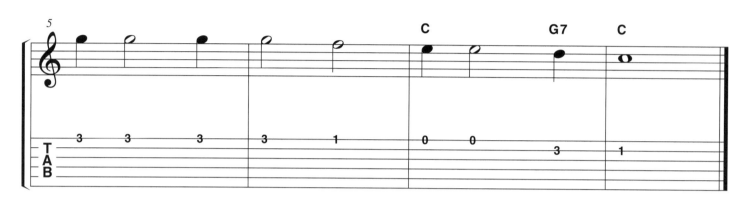

Dynamics may change in the course of a song. When this happens, be sure to exaggerate the loudness and softness of the music.

Under the Sea

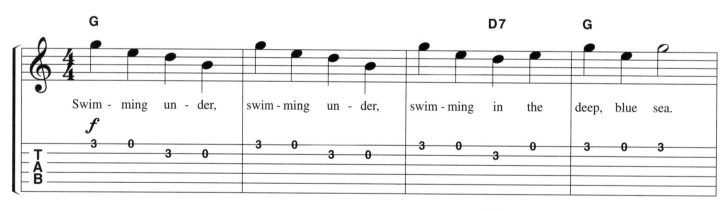

Swim - ming un - der, swim - ming un - der, swim - ming in the deep, blue sea.

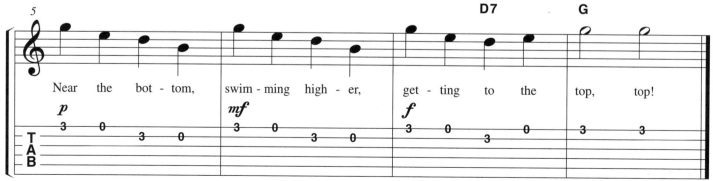

Near the bot - tom, swim - ming high - er, get - ting to the top, top!

12 Crusader's Hymn

German

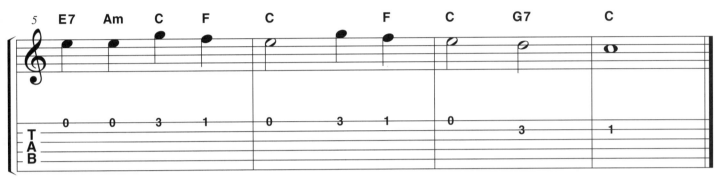

13 My Dreydel

S.E. Goldfarb, S.S. Grossman

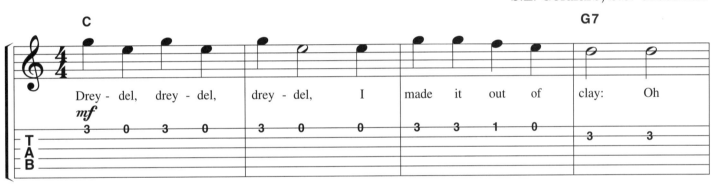

Drey - del, drey - del, drey - del, I made it out of clay: Oh

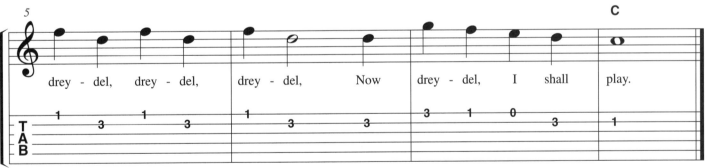

drey - del, drey - del, drey - del, Now drey - del, I shall play.

Write in the missing TAB numbers. Be sure that they line up with the notes on the staff. Then play the example.

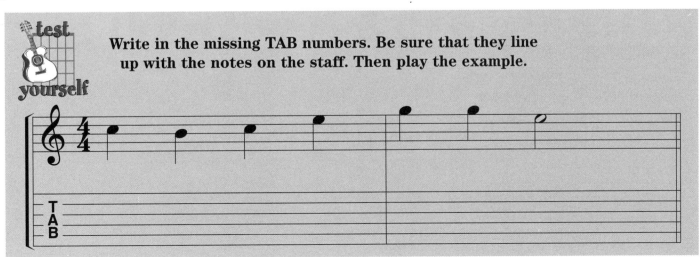

NOTES ON THE THIRD STRING

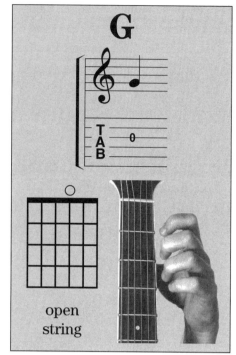

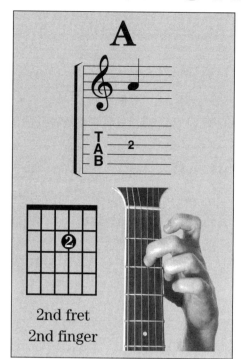

Third String Warm-up

Aura Lee (14)

Traditional

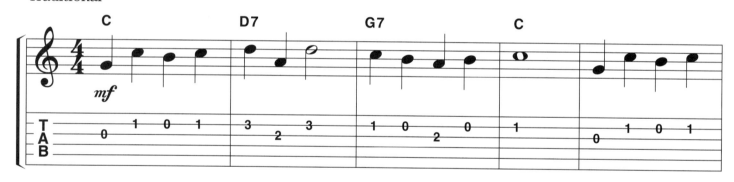

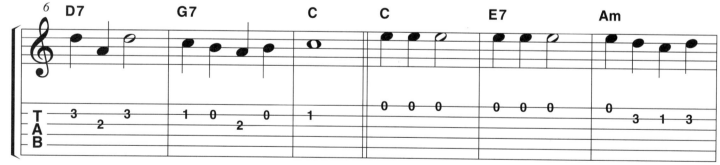

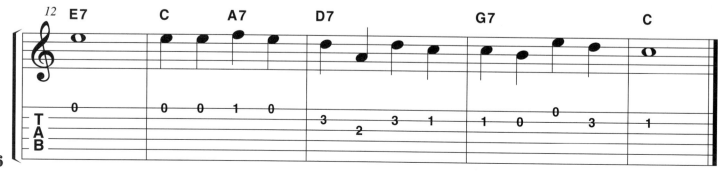

Pick-up notes are notes that come before the first complete measure. The beats in the pick-up measure and the last measure usually add up to one complete measure.

15 The Snake Charmer

Traditional

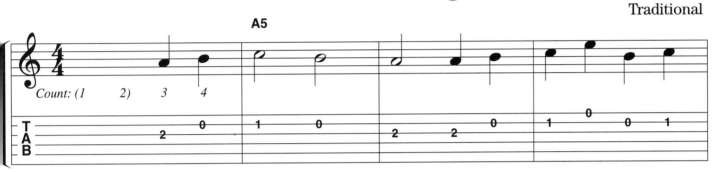

Count: (1   2)   3   4

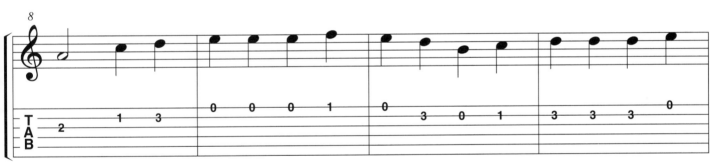

Circle the measures that contain an incorrect number of beats.

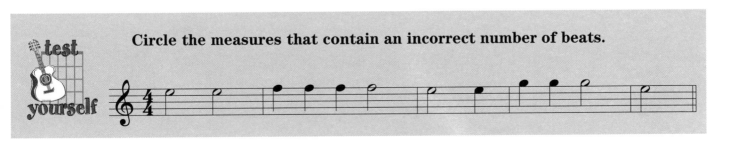

¾ TIME

Music with a ¾ **time signature** gets three beats per measure. Each beat is equal to one quarter note.

DOTTED HALF NOTES

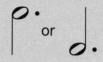

A dot placed after a note increases the value of the note by one half of its value. The **dotted half note** gets *three* beats.

♩ (2 beats) + ♩ (1 beat) = ♩. (3 beats)

Vive l'amour (16)

French Melody

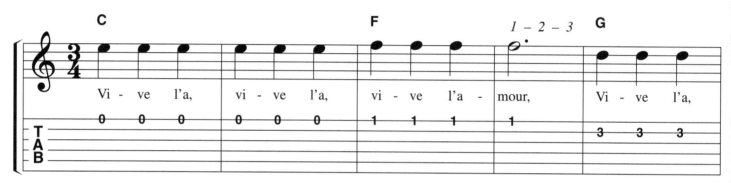

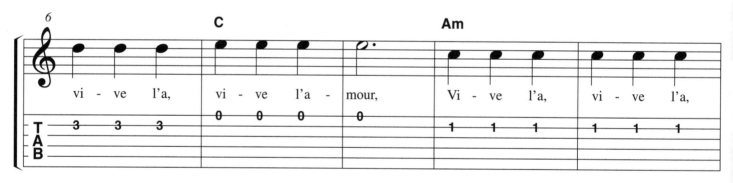

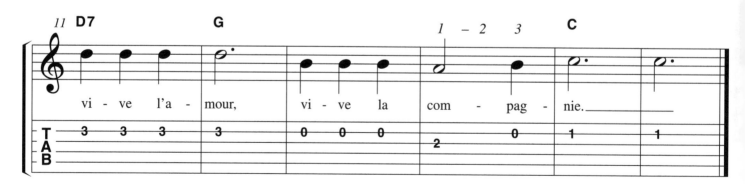

 When playing notes that get two or more beats be sure that the note sounds for the correct amount of beats. If you lift up your left-hand finger too quickly, the sound will stop. If an open string is even touched lightly, the sound will stop.

TIES

A **tie** connects two notes that are on the same line or space. Play the *first note only*, allowing it to sound for the combined value of both notes. The parentheses in the tablature indicates that the tied note is held and not played again.

(17) When the Saints Go Marching In

Traditional American

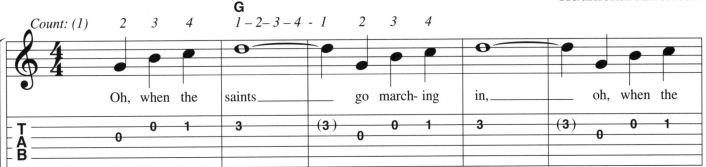

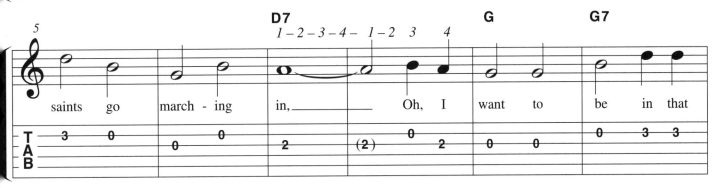

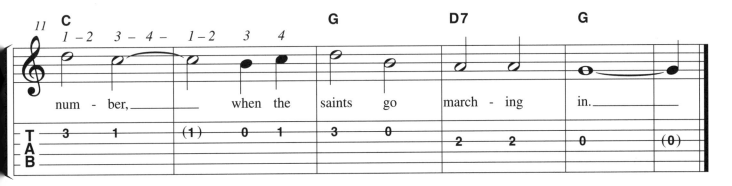

OCTAVES

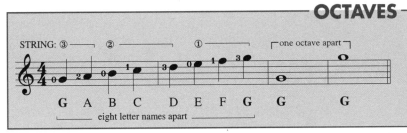

An **octave** consists of two notes that share the same name, and are eight letter names apart. You have now learned two *different* "G" notes.

Octave Warm-up

19

CHORD PREPARATION

Notes that are stacked on top of each other are to be played at the same time.
Use a downstroke to strum quickly through the notes.

In this example, you may rest your pick on the first string after playing the stacked notes.

A **chord** is three or more notes played together.

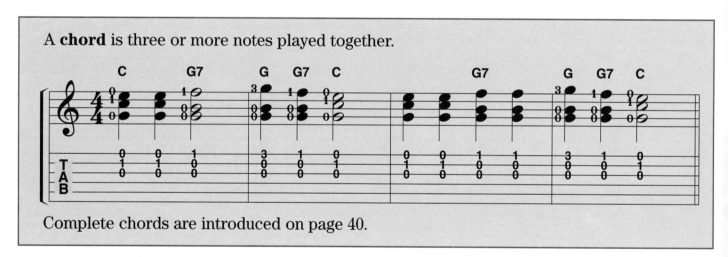

Complete chords are introduced on page 40.

Chord Warm-up

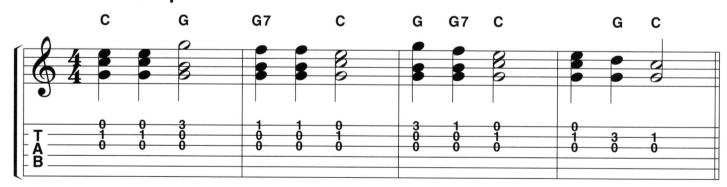

 Learn to identify each three-note chord by letter name and by the way the chord looks in music notation.

18 Down in the Valley
Traditional

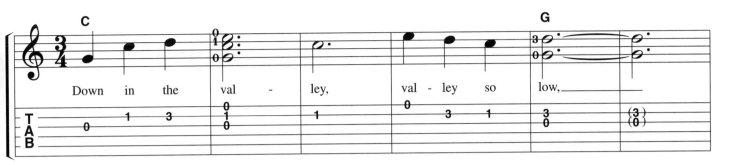

Down in the val - ley, val - ley so low,

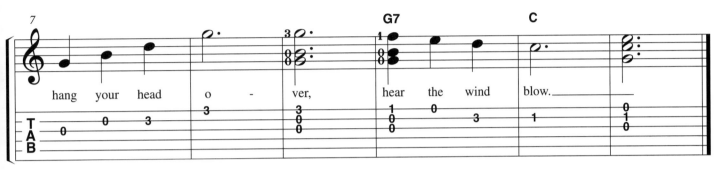

hang your head o - ver, hear the wind blow.

19 The Cuckoo
German Folksong

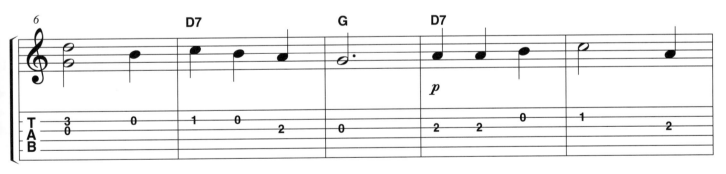

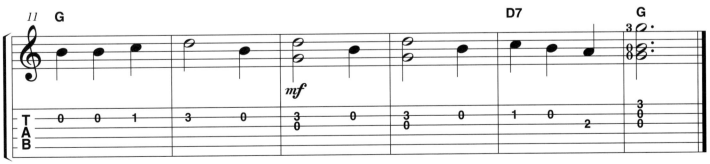

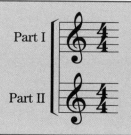

DUETS

Part I

Part II

A **duet** is a piece of music for two performers. The ability to play well with others is one of the top requirements of a good musician. Accurate rhythm is very important because both players must be in the same place at the same time. Learn to play both Parts I and II of each duet.

Ode to Joy ⑳

Beethoven's Ninth Symphony

STUDENT DUET

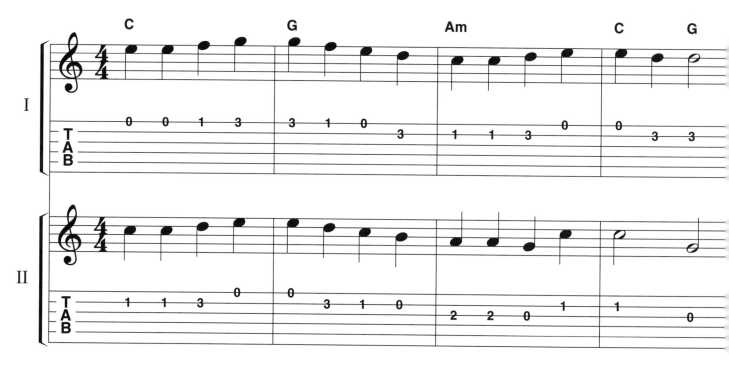

Note: Students may prefer to learn the following rhythm in Part I, measures 4, 8, 16, 20 by rote.

22

 Each day, play the eight notes you have learned both ascending and descending for one minute. Gradually increase the tempo while maintaining a steady beat with a legato sound.

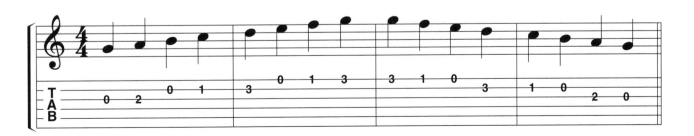

NOTES ON THE FOURTH STRING

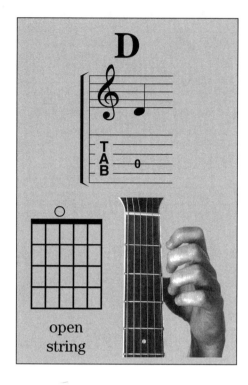

D

open string

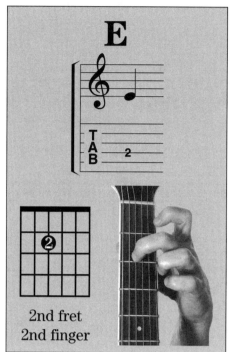

E

2nd fret
2nd finger

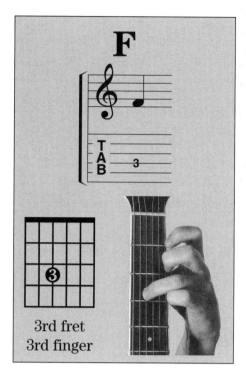

F

3rd fret
3rd finger

Fourth String Warm-up

Au clair de la lune ㉑
French Folksong

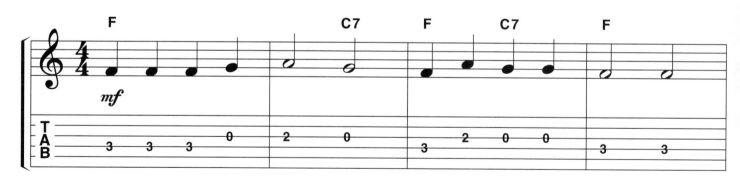

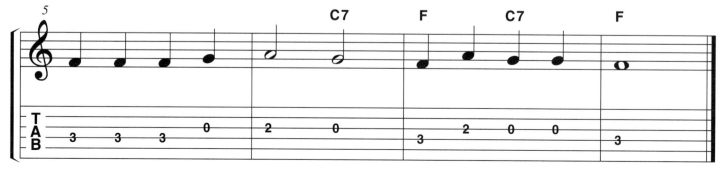

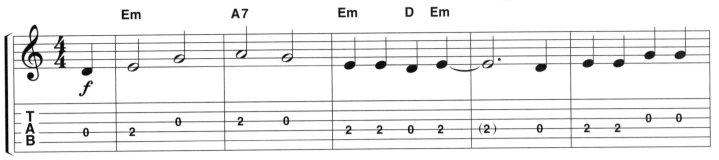

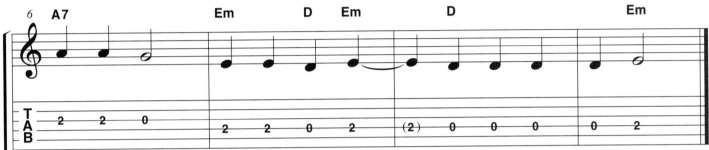

(23) **Reuben and Rachel**

Music by William Gooch
Lyrics by Harry Birch

use the fourth finger

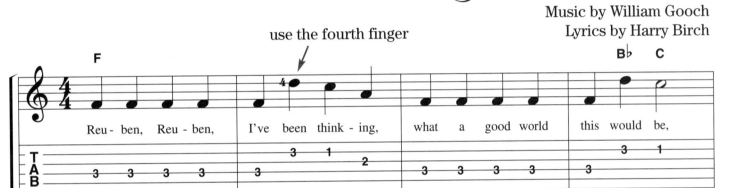

Reu - ben, Reu - ben, I've been think - ing, what a good world this would be,

if the boys were all trans - port - ed, far be - yond the North - ern Sea!

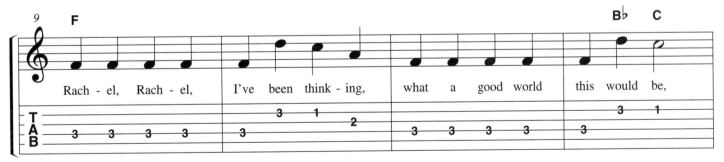

Rach - el, Rach - el, I've been think - ing, what a good world this would be,

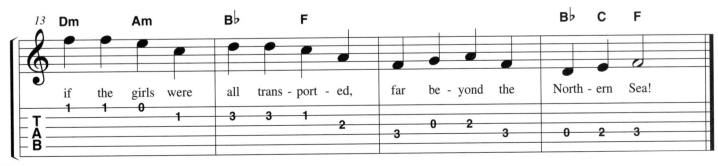

if the girls were all trans - port - ed, far be - yond the North - ern Sea!

Five Hundred Miles (24)
Traditional Song of the British Isles

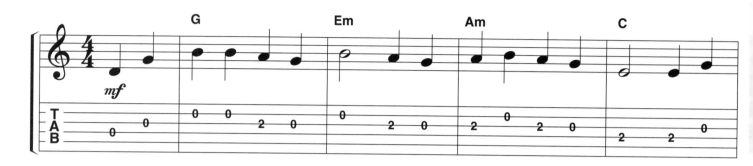

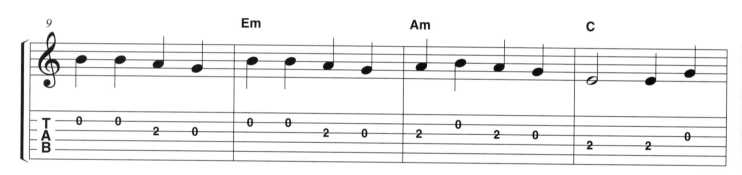

Note Review Chart:
Each day, play the eleven notes you have learned both ascending and descending for one minute, saying the names of the notes as you play them.

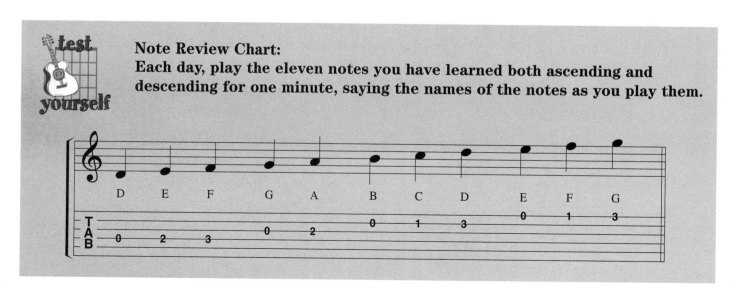

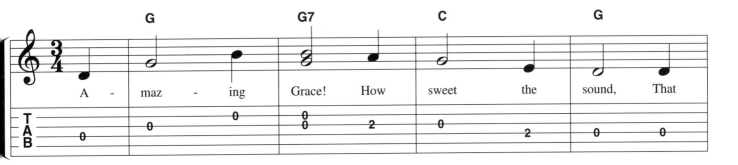

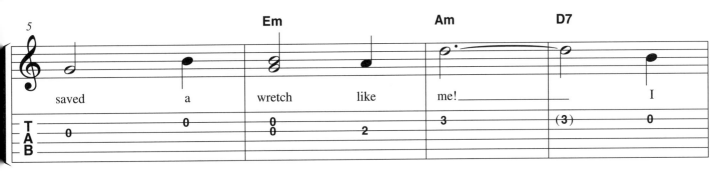

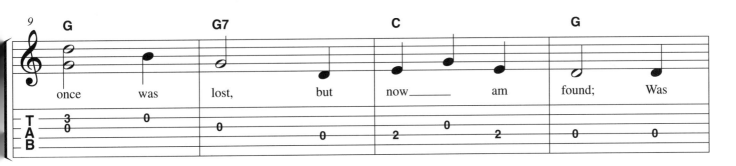

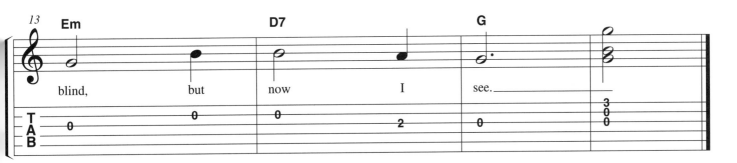

 When playing two-note chords (as in measures 2, 6, and 9), you may rest your pick on the first string (instead of trying to miss it).

A quarter note can be divided into two equal parts called **eighth notes**. A single eighth note has a **flag** (♪). Two or more eighth notes may be connected by a **beam** (♫).

♪ = ½ beat   ♫ = 1 beat   ♫♫ = 2 beats

You may use alternating downstrokes and upstrokes at this time. Move your pick down (⊓) and up (V) as you play eighth notes. Count: 1 + (and) 2 + 3 + 4 + throughout.

Study in Eighth Notes

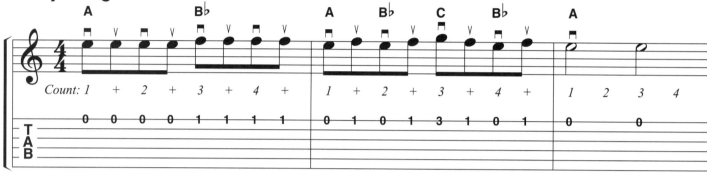

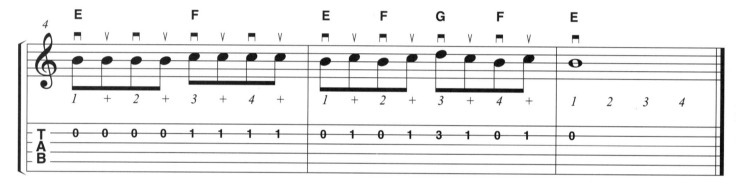

French Minuet

Jean-Philippe Rameau

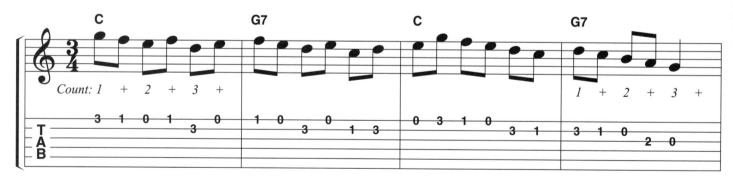

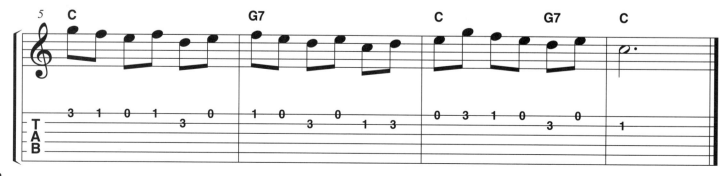

G1

Learn the correct notes and rhythm of each song before using **alternate picking** (⊓ ∨ ⊓ ∨) *on eighth notes. A good way to begin is to use alternate picking only on repeated eighth notes, or notes that are all on the same string. Eventually you will want to use alternate picking on all eighth-note groups.*

(27) A Minor Detour

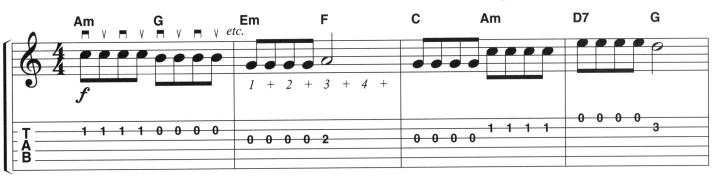

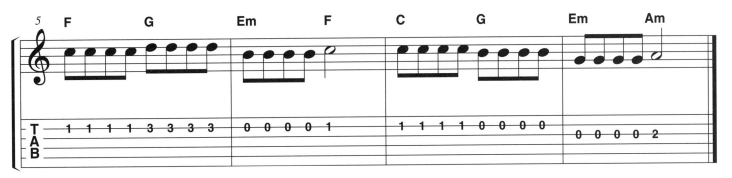

 **Fill in the blanks with the correct number of beats for each note value.**

o = _____ beat(s)   𝅗𝅥. = _____ beat(s)   𝅗𝅥 = _____ beat(s)

♩ = _____ beat(s)   ♪ = _____ beat(s)

Test your rhythm knowledge.

Tap a steady beat with your foot (or use a metronome ♩=60). Using any open string, play the four lines of the Rhythm Chart, counting aloud. Always continue to the next line without stopping. Mix up the rhythms until you are comfortable with any combination.

Rhythm Chart

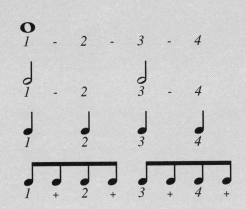

Frère Jacques (28)

Traditional French Round*

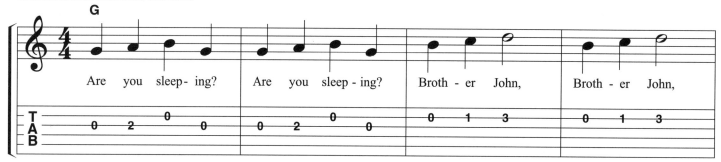

Are you sleep-ing? Are you sleep-ing? Broth - er John, Broth - er John,

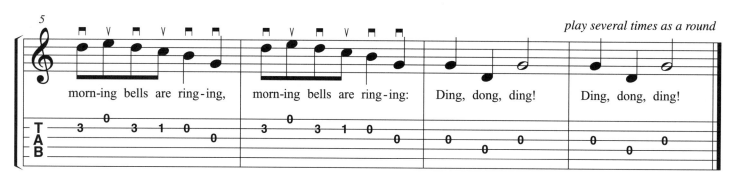

play several times as a round

morn-ing bells are ring-ing, morn-ing bells are ring-ing: Ding, dong, ding! Ding, dong, ding!

Frère Jacques may be played as a round with a second guitarist.
As the first guitarist plays measure three, the second guitarist starts to play.

Kooper Keeper (29)

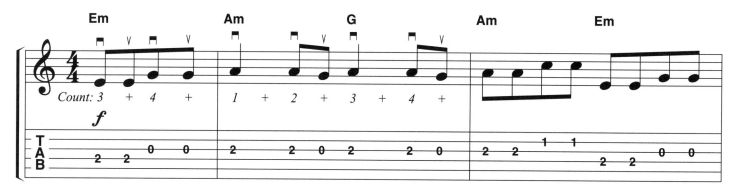

Count: 3 + 4 + 1 + 2 + 3 + 4 +

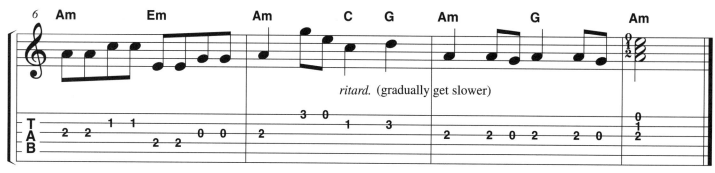

ritard. (gradually get slower)

ARPEGGIOS

arpeggio   block chords

An **arpeggio** is a chord in which the notes are played one after another, instead of at the same time. Keep your left-hand fingers down as you glide your pick from one string to another.

Chord Study

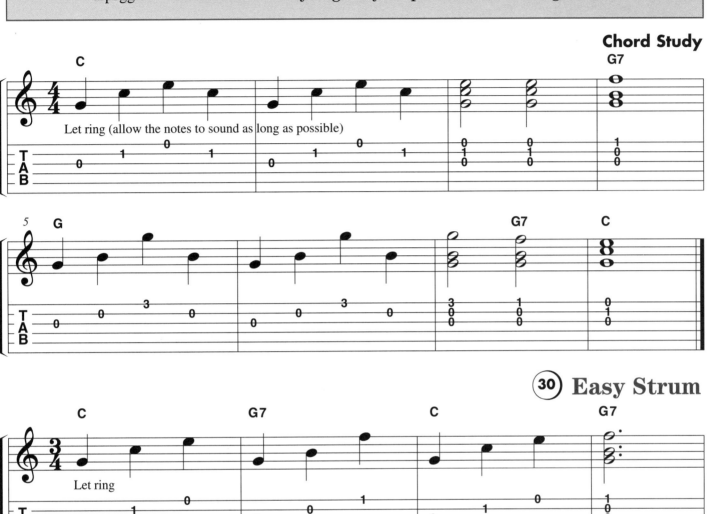

Let ring (allow the notes to sound as long as possible)

30 Easy Strum

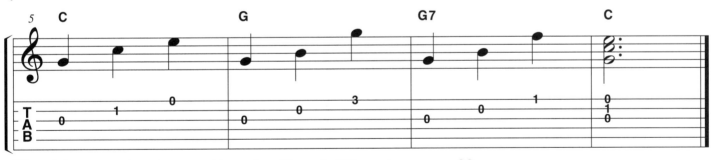

Let ring

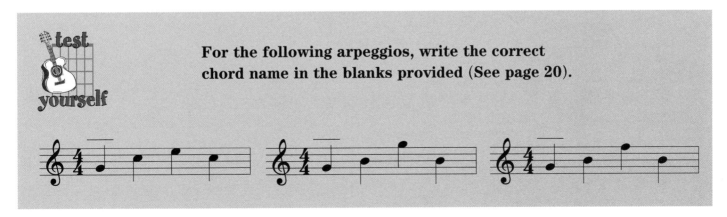

Use this arpeggio strum pattern for *French Minuet* on page 28.

For the following arpeggios, write the correct chord name in the blanks provided (See page 20).

Pachelbel Canon ㉛

Johann Pachelbel

STUDENT DUET

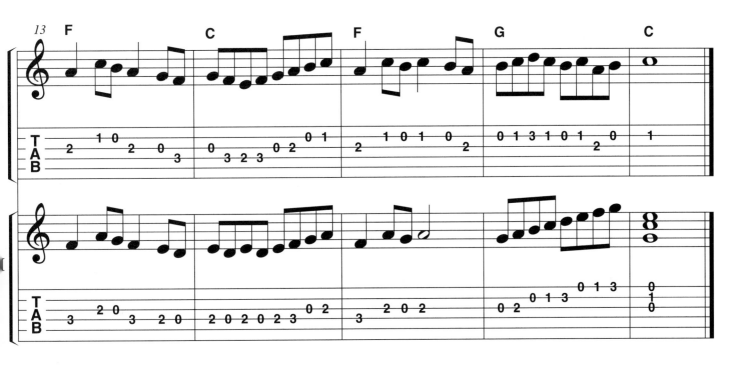

(32) **Morning**

Edvard Grieg

NOTES ON THE FIFTH STRING

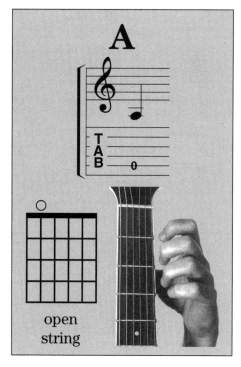

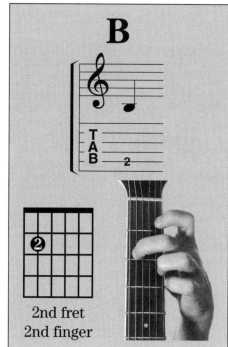

A — open string

B — 2nd fret 2nd finger

C — 3rd fret 3rd finger

Fifth String Warm-up

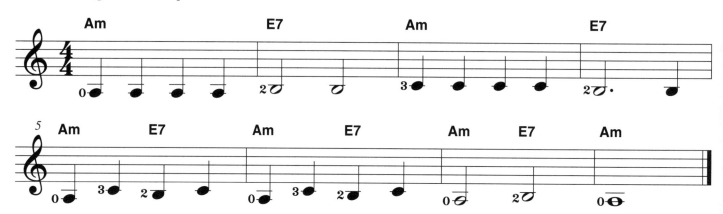

LEDGER LINES

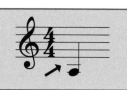

Ledger lines are needed for low or high notes that do not fit on the staff.

Notice that the fingering is the same for the notes you have learned on the fourth and fifth strings. Play these notes while saying the note names aloud.

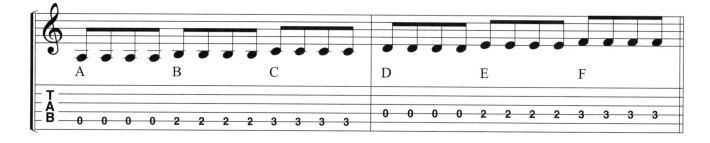

A   B   C   D   E   F

G

Surf Boogie

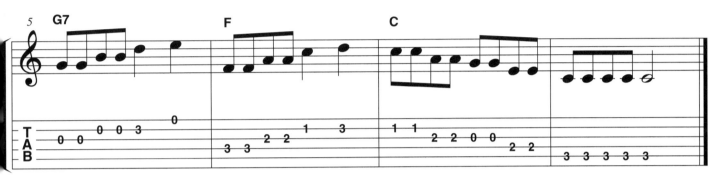

Train to Oz

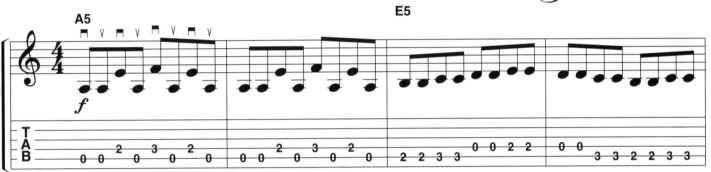

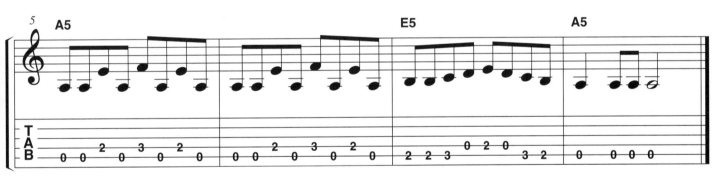

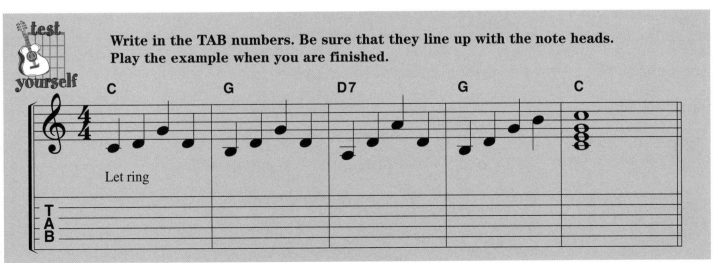

Write in the TAB numbers. Be sure that they line up with the note heads.
Play the example when you are finished.

NOTES ON THE SIXTH STRING

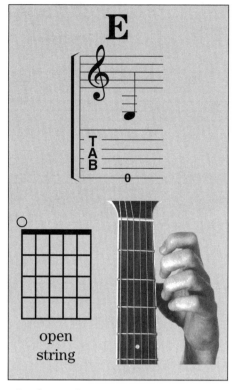

E

open
string

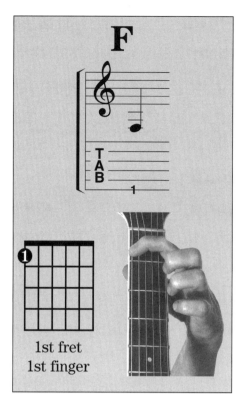

F

1st fret
1st finger

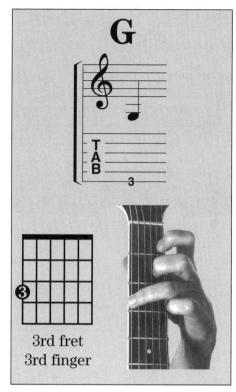

G

3rd fret
3rd finger

Sixth String Warm-up

N.C. (No Chord) means do not strum any chords until the next chord name appears.

R&B (35)

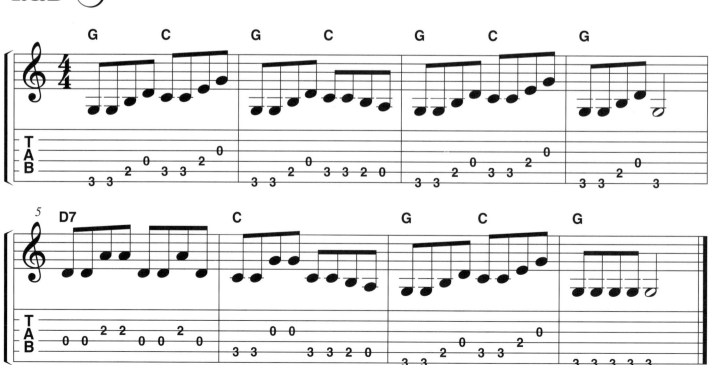

A **fermata** indicates that a note or a rest should be held longer than its normal value.

(36) **EZ Blues**

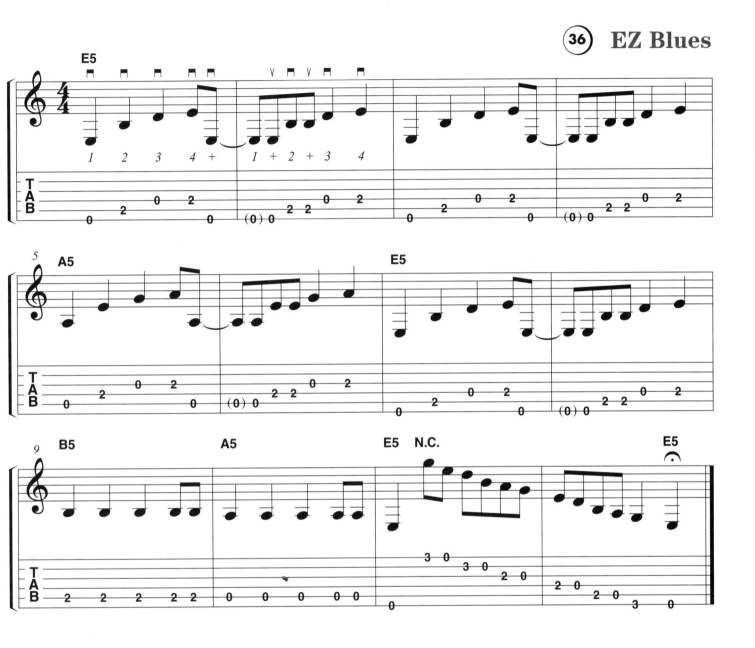

NATURAL NOTES IN FIRST POSITION

The following chart lists all of the notes that you have learned. Notice that the first finger plays all of the first fret notes; the second finger plays all of the second fret notes; and the third finger plays all of the third fret notes. The fourth finger will play all of the notes on the fourth fret. This is referred to as playing in **First Position**.

SHARPS

A **sharp** (#) *raises* the pitch of a note by one fret (one half step). The sharp symbol stays in effect until the end of a measure.

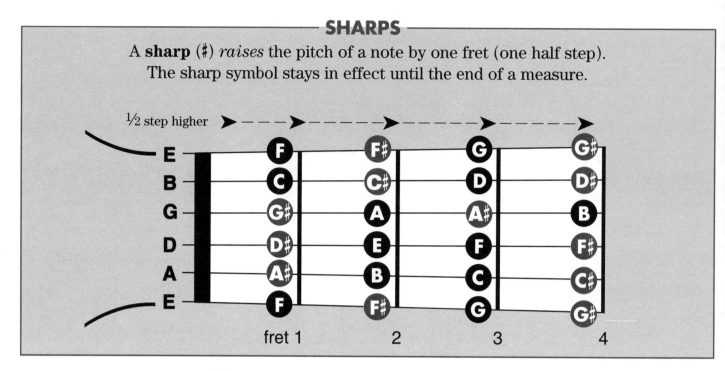

Classical Study (37)

Ferdinand Carulli (arranged)

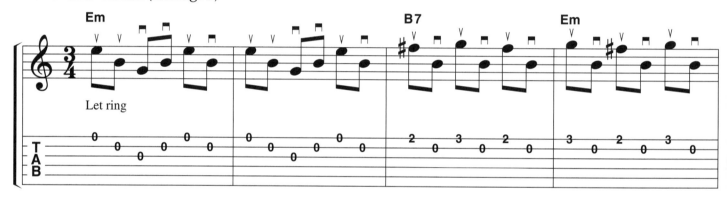

 When a sharp is added to an open string note, play the new note on the first fret.

38

NATURALS

A **natural** (♮) *cancels* a sharp or a flat (page 65) previously used.

(38) **Top Secret**

*Strum the chord slowly.

REPEAT SIGNS

Music enclosed by **repeat signs** is to be played again.
A repeat sign may be omitted in the beginning of a song.

Daily Power Study

*Notice the new location for note B. Many notes on the guitar can be found in two or more places.

CHORDS

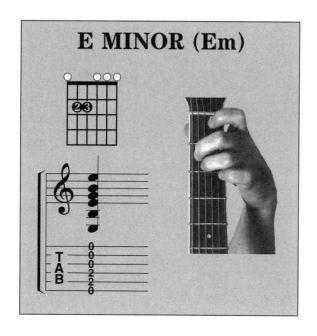

E MINOR (Em)

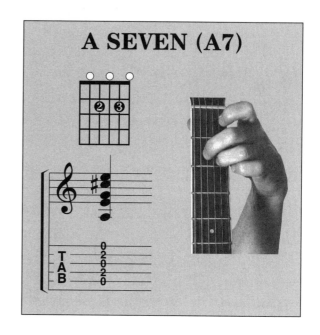

A SEVEN (A7)

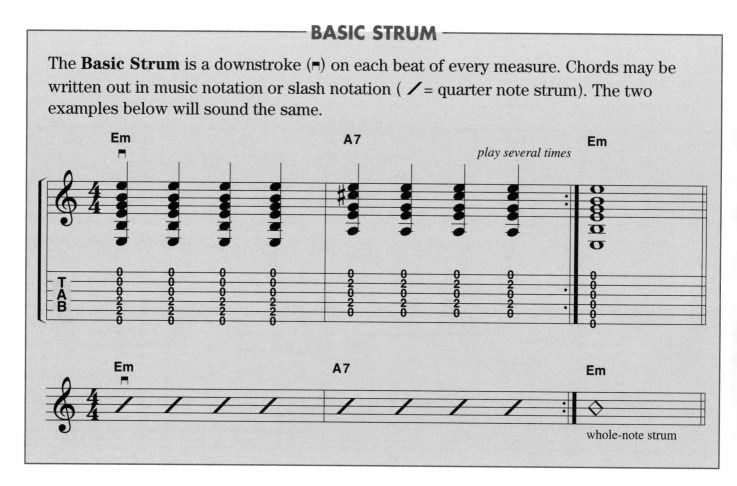

BASIC STRUM

The **Basic Strum** is a downstroke (⊓) on each beat of every measure. Chords may be written out in music notation or slash notation (╱ = quarter note strum). The two examples below will sound the same.

Complete chords include four, five, and six strings. If a string is not played open or is not played by the left hand, do not strum the string with your right hand. Therefore, A7 is a five-string chord.

CHANGING CHORDS

- Memorize the location of the left-hand fingers for each new chord. Notice that Em and A7 have similar left-hand shapes.
- When changing from one chord to the next, move your left hand (and fingers) quickly so your right hand can strum with a steady beat (without stopping or hesitating).
- Practice the following example several times without stopping the pulse of the music. Count out loud as you strum evenly.

 Whenever possible, learn both the melody and the chords to a song. Strum with a steady beat, especially when changing from one chord to another. For songs with lyrics, practice singing as you strum the chords. Slash notation may be placed above the staff, as in "Two-Chord Blues."

(39) Two-Chord Blues

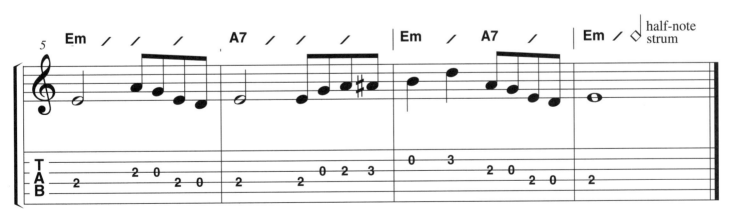

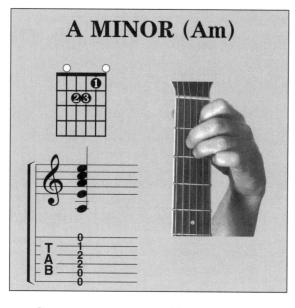

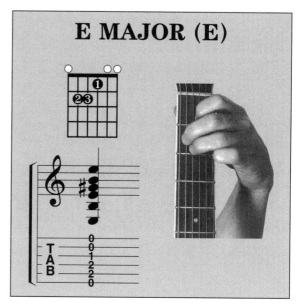

Lullaby (40)
Latvian Folksong

Lul - la - by, my ba - by,_____ soft - ly

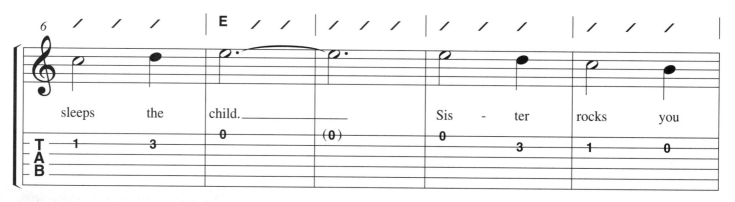

sleeps the child._____ Sis - ter rocks you

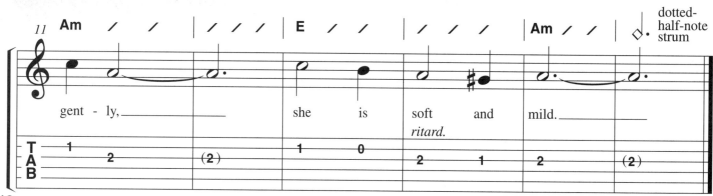

gent - ly,_____ she is soft and mild._____

ritard.

dotted-
half-note
strum

42

THE ROOT STRUM

Every chord has a **root** note, which is the letter name of the chord. For example, the root of Am is A. To play the **Root Strum** pattern, play the *lowest-pitched root* on beat one. Let the root note ring as you strum the treble strings (③, ②, and ①) on the remaining beats.

Root Strum on Em and A7 in $\frac{4}{4}$ time.

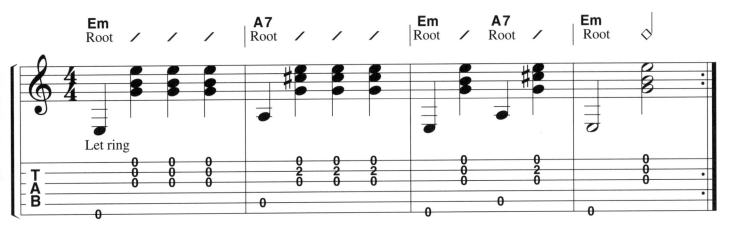

Now play *Two-Chord Blues* on page 41 using the Root Strum.

Root Strum on Am and E in $\frac{3}{4}$ time.

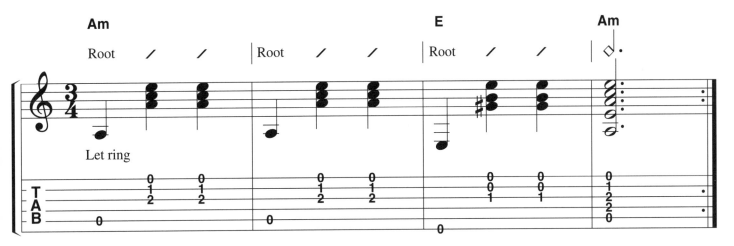

Now play *Lullaby* on page 42 using the Root Strum.

Be sure to let all notes ring out (Let ring) as long as possible when strumming chords.
Use the "Natural Notes In First Position Chart" on page 37 to help you identify all of the lowest-root notes.

Everybody's Strum & Play Guitar Chords (G1042) has many valuable technique tips and playing hints to help you learn to strum chords quickly and easily.

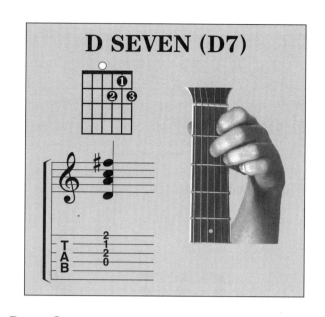

Basic Strum

Root Strum

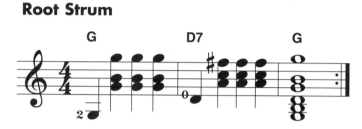

 Guide Fingers are fingers that keep gentle contact with the strings when changing between chords. For example, keep your third finger on the first string when changing from G to D7.

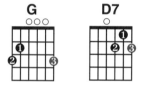

Hush, Little Baby 41

Carolina Folksong

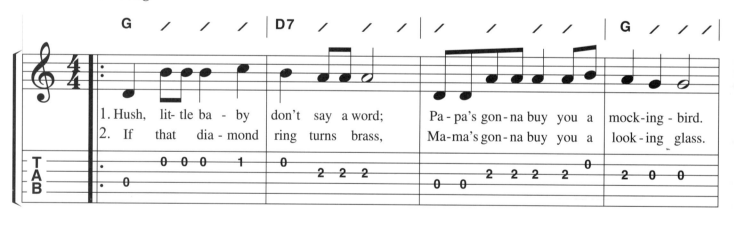

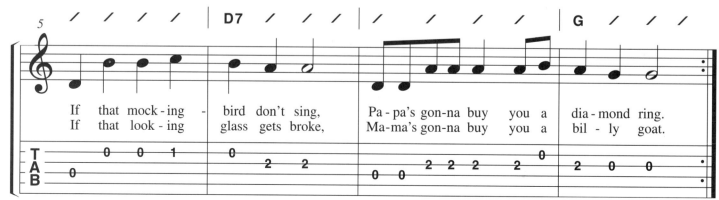

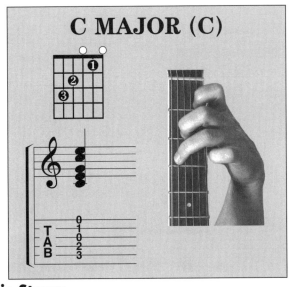

Basic Strum

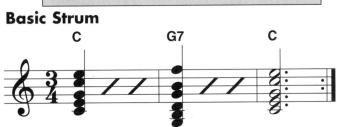

Root Strum

 You may practice chords without left-hand pressure at first. Keep the relaxed-looking form as you add pressure. Looking ahead to the next chord can help you change chords more easily. When playing chords, begin strumming in the first complete measure.

(42) **Oh Where Has My Little Dog Gone?**

German Folksong

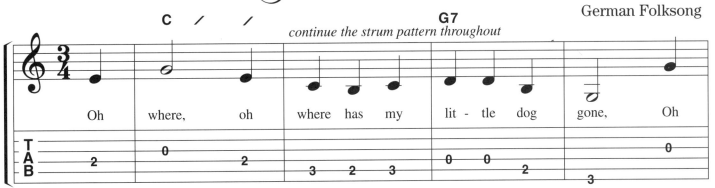

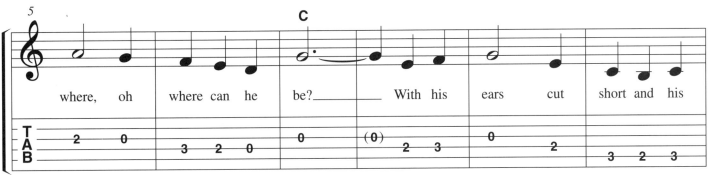

Common Fingers *are fingers that remain in position when changing chords. For example, keep your first finger in the same place for both the C and D7 chords.*

Yankee Doodle 43

Traditional

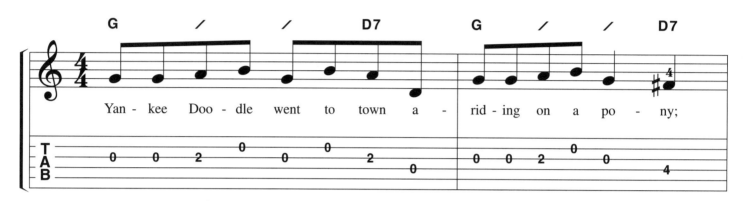

Yan - kee Doo - dle went to town a - rid - ing on a po - ny;

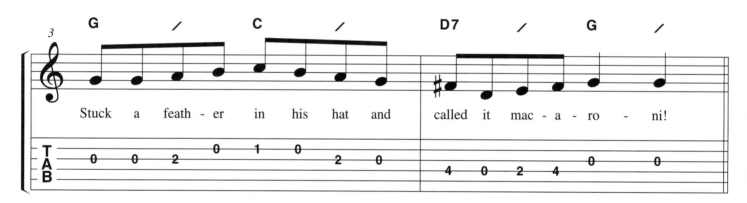

Stuck a feath - er in his hat and called it mac - a - ro - ni!

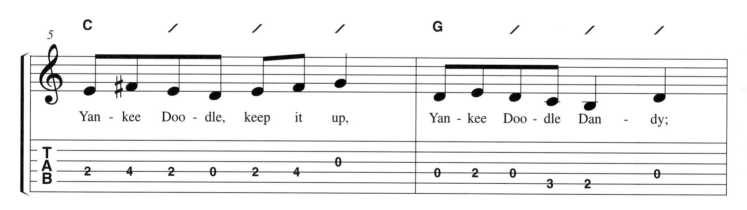

Yan - kee Doo - dle, keep it up, Yan - kee Doo - dle Dan - dy;

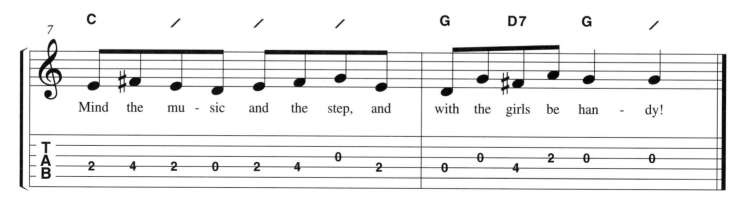

Mind the mu - sic and the step, and with the girls be han - dy!

G1C

Alternate fingerings may be used with chords to allow use of common fingers. When playing "Simple Gifts", use the alternate fingering for Em as shown.

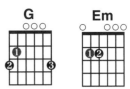

(44) Simple Gifts

Traditional

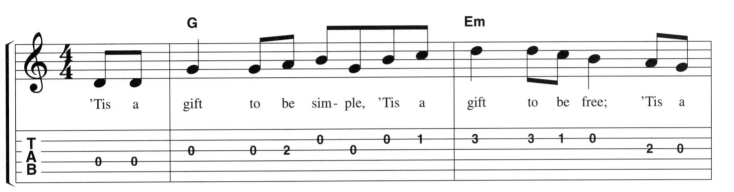

'Tis a gift to be sim- ple, 'Tis a gift to be free; 'Tis a

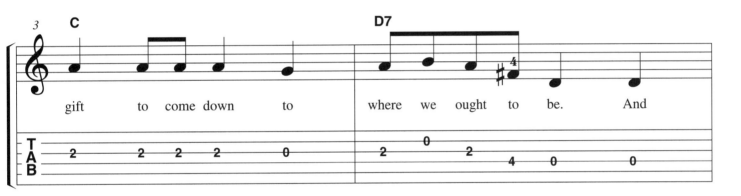

gift to come down to where we ought to be. And

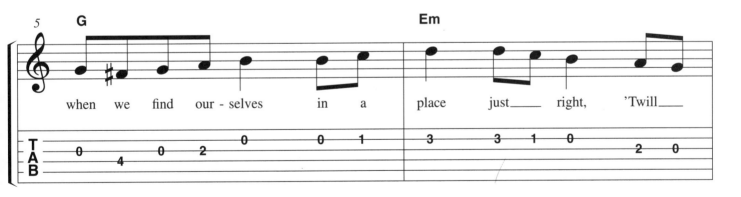

when we find our - selves in a place just___ right, 'Twill___

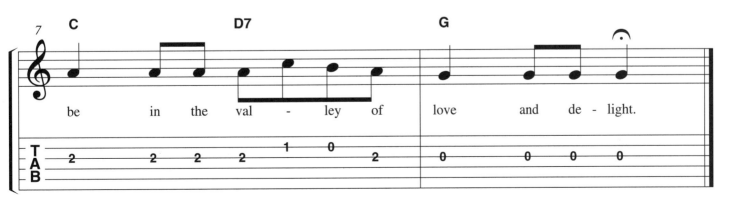

be in the val - ley of love and de - light.

Folías de España (45)

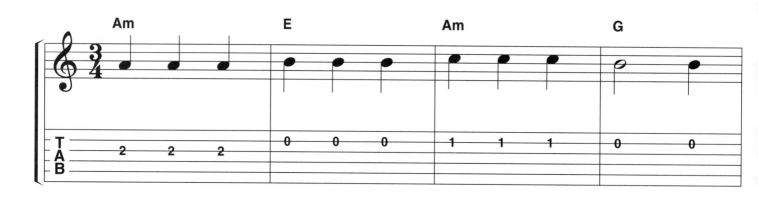

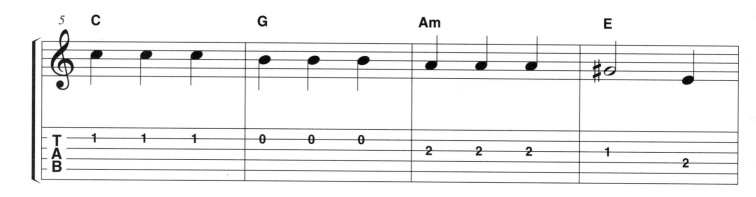

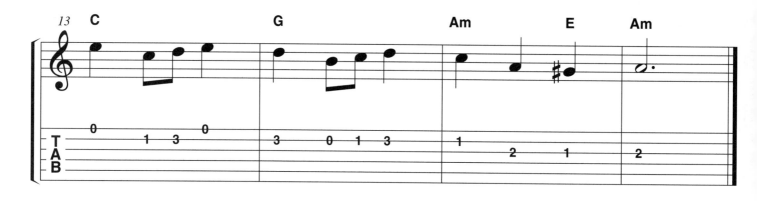

 Be sure to mentally prepare before starting to play a melody in ¾ time. Count several measures of 3, slightly accenting beat 1, until you feel the rhythm of ¾ time.

46 On Top of Old Smoky

Traditional

Now that you have learned eight basic chords, you can strum an accompaniment to many of the songs in the beginning of the book. See pages 110–111 for a complete listing of all the chords used in this book.

DOTTED QUARTER NOTES

The **dotted quarter note** gets one and one half beats.   ♩. = 1½ beats

The note following a dotted quarter note will often be an eighth note (♪).

♩ (1 beat) + ♪ (½ beat) = ♩. (1½ beats)

Lines 2 and 3 should sound the same.

Dotted Quarter-Note Warm-up

London Bridge (47)

Traditional

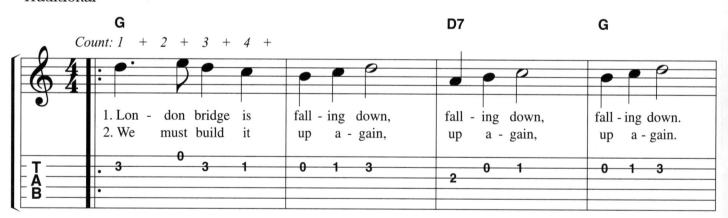

1. Lon - don bridge is   fall - ing down,   fall - ing down,   fall - ing down.
2. We   must build it   up   a - gain,   up   a - gain,   up   a - gain.

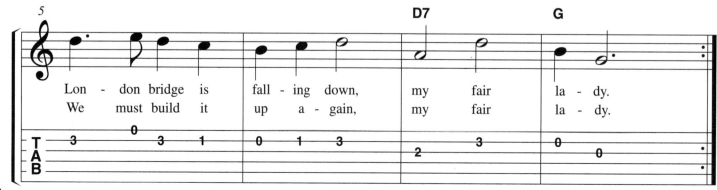

Lon - don bridge is   fall - ing down,   my   fair   la - dy.
We   must build it   up   a - gain,   my   fair   la - dy.

50

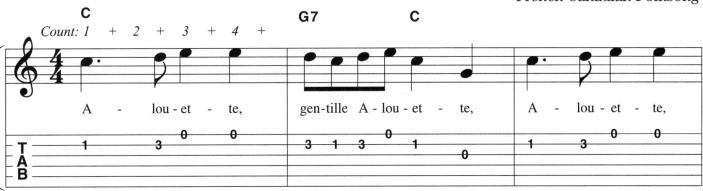

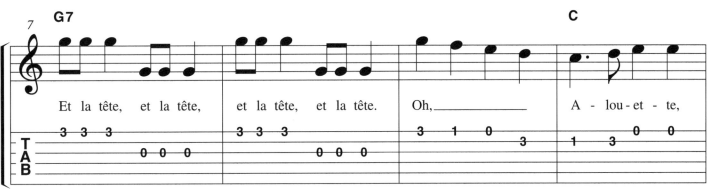

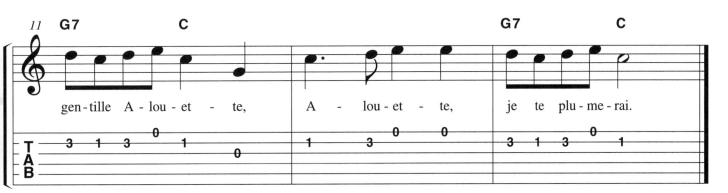

Write in the counting for the melody below. Include all downbeats (numbers) and upbeats (+'s). Then play while counting aloud.

America, the Beautiful (49)

Katharine Lee Bates, Samuel A. Ward

STUDENT DUET

Lyrics: O beau - ti - ful for spa - cious skies, for am - ber waves of grain, For pur - ple moun - tain maj - es - ties a - bove the fruit - ed plain! A - mer - i - ca! A - mer - i - ca! God shed His grace on thee, And

G1048

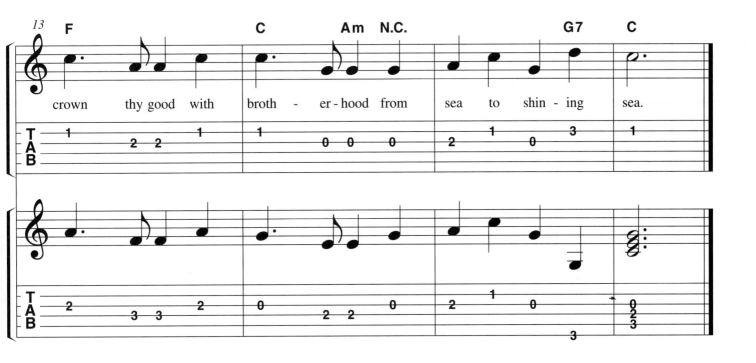

crown thy good with broth - er - hood from sea to shin - ing sea.

50 Half-Step Blues

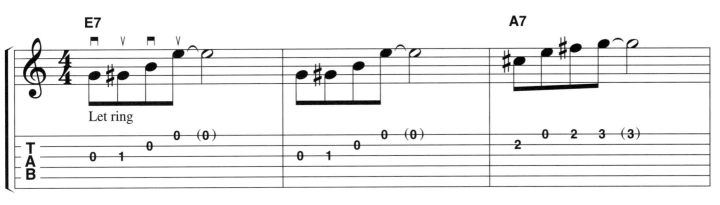

Let ring

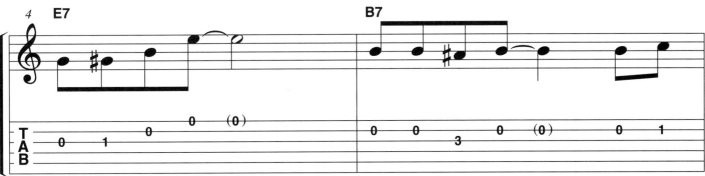

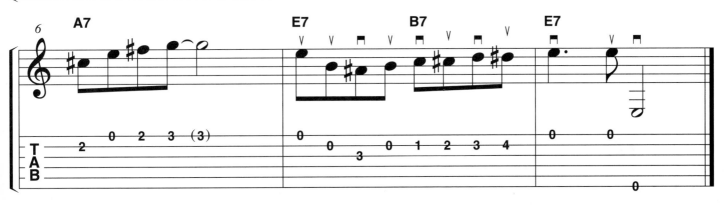

NOTES ON THE FIFTH FRET

NEW NOTE A

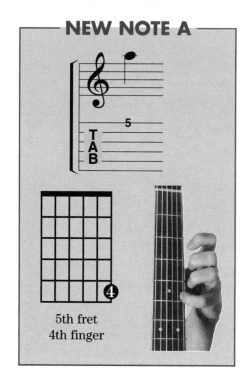

5th fret
4th finger

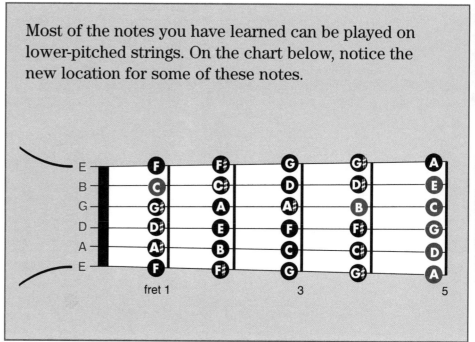

Most of the notes you have learned can be played on lower-pitched strings. On the chart below, notice the new location for some of these notes.

Eastbound Trail (51)

Korean Folksong

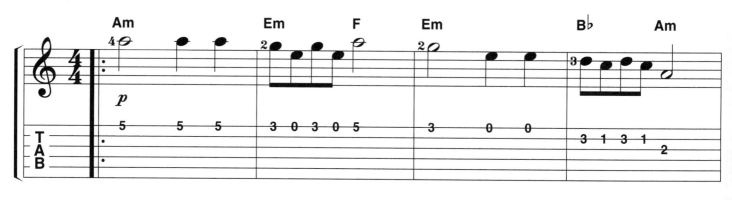

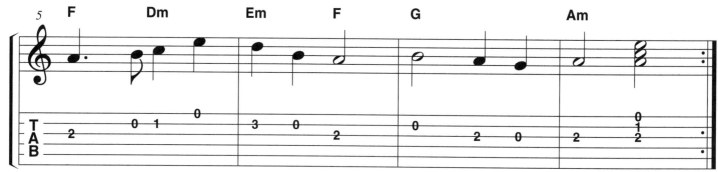

 Notice the left-hand finger numbers do not always match the fret a note is played on. As you learn more notes on higher-numbered frets you will see that this happens much more often.

G

52 Coconut Grove

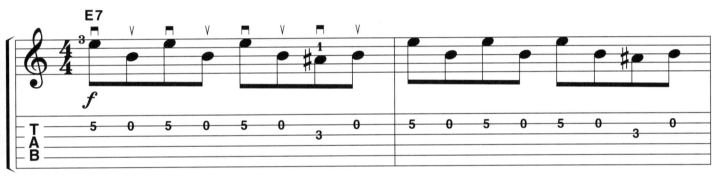

53 Cyclone

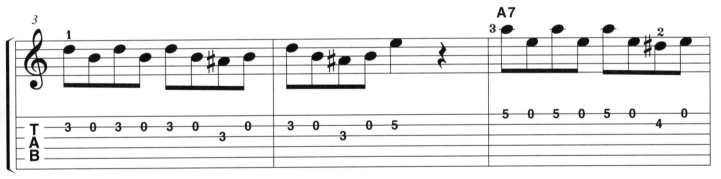

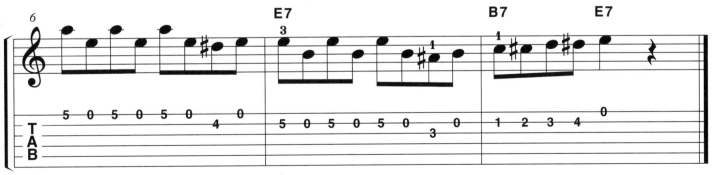

"Cyclone" is an example of a song that can look rather difficult in notation, but becomes much easier to play when looking at the tablature.

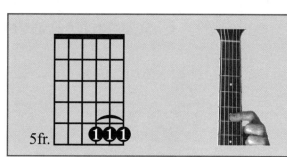

THE BARRE

A **barre** is when a left-hand finger holds down *more than one* note at a time.

In the last measure of *Greensleeves*, you will play a barre at the fifth fret on strings one, two, and three.

5fr.

Greensleeves (54)

English Folksong

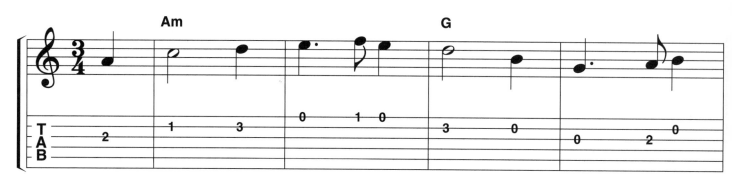

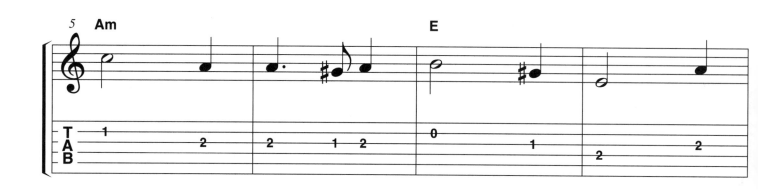

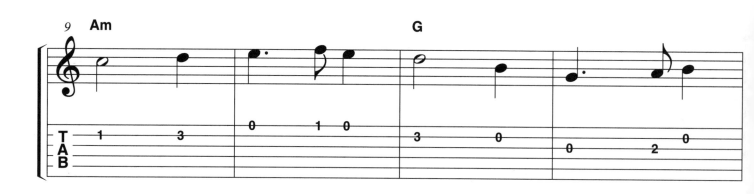

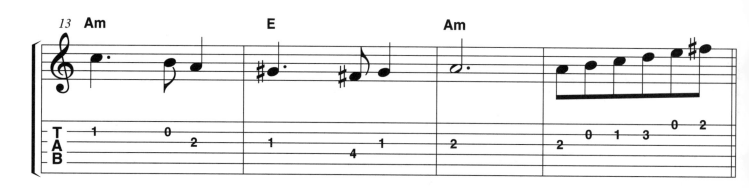

56

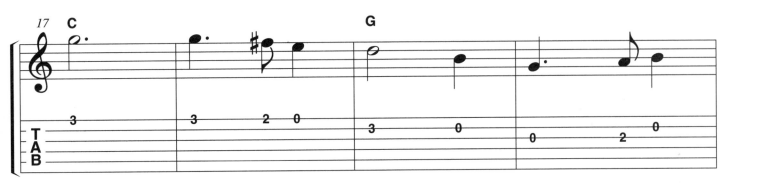

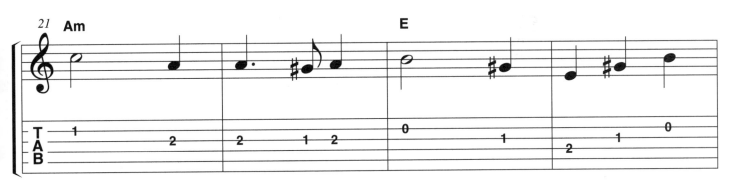

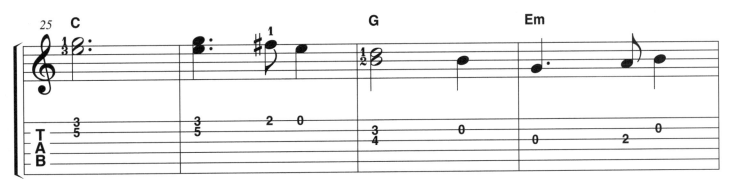

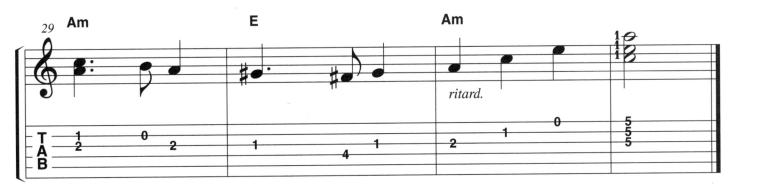

 Use open strings to your advantage to help you change positions smoothly. Try this technique in measures 31–32. The pulse must always remain steady.

POWER CHORDS

Power chords are used in many popular and rock songs. These chords usually consist of two notes, which are called the root and the fifth. Often heard with distortion on electric guitar, the unique sound of power chords makes them fun to play.

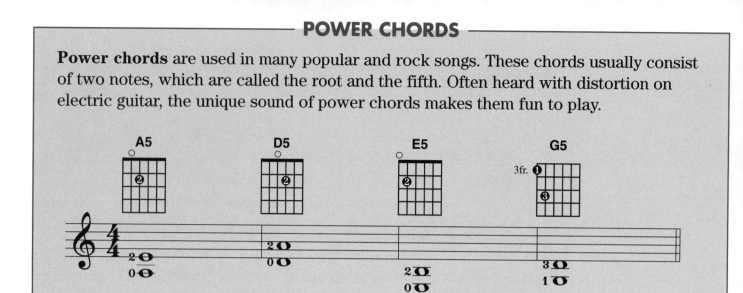

Power Play (55)

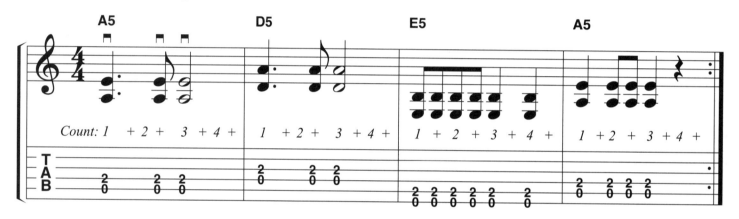

Power Play uses power chords with one open string.

Moving Around (56)

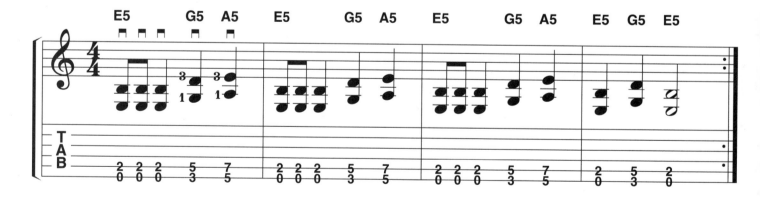

"Moving Around" uses the G5 power chord which has no open strings. This feature makes the G5 shape movable. Once you can get a good sound strumming the G5 chord, use the guide-finger technique to move your left hand up to A5 on the fifth fret.

The A5 power chord may be played with or without open strings.

G1(

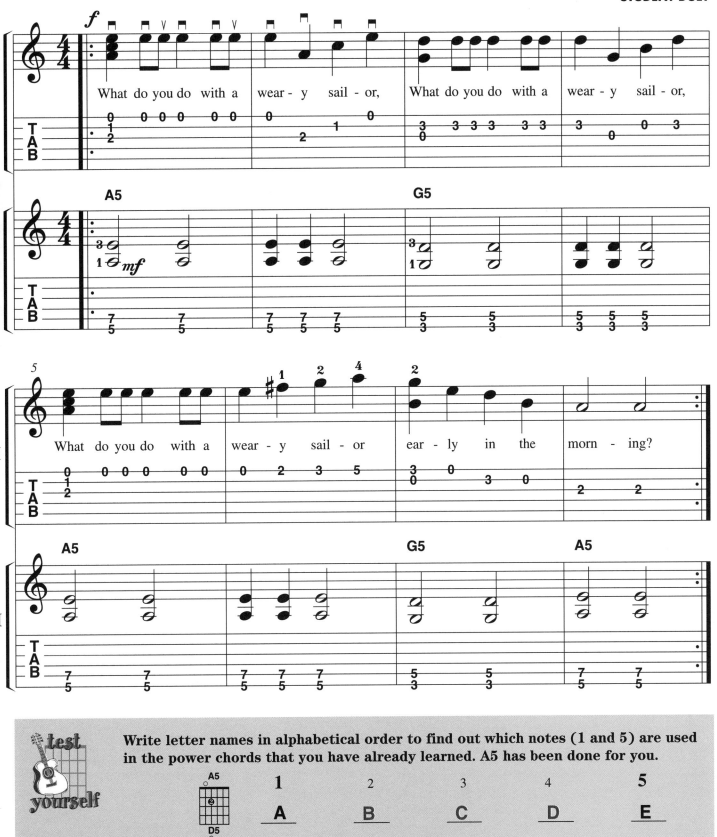

Lyrics (melody, top staff):

What do you do with a wear-y sail-or, What do you do with a wear-y sail-or,

What do you do with a wear-y sail-or ear-ly in the morn-ing?

Chords (bottom staff): A5, G5, A5, G5, A5

Write letter names in alphabetical order to find out which notes (1 and 5) are used in the power chords that you have already learned. A5 has been done for you.

	1	2	3	4	5
A5	A	B	C	D	E
D5	D				
E5	E				
G5	G				

48

59

A **rest** is a moment of *silence* in music. Each note value has an equal rest value.

whole	*half*	*quarter*	*eighth*
𝅝 ▬ = 4 beats	𝅗𝅥 ▬ = 2 beats	♩ 𝄽 = 1 beat	♪ 𝄾 = ½ beat

***Dampen** the strings when necessary. Releasing the pressure of a left-hand finger will stop a string from vibrating. To dampen an open string, use the fingers of the left hand to lightly touch the vibrating strings.*

There's Always Time to Rest (58)

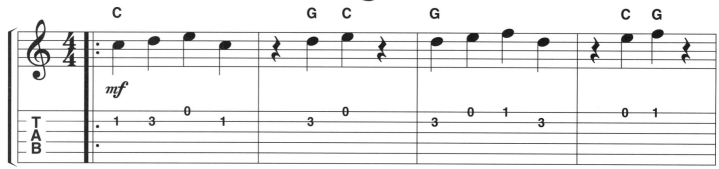

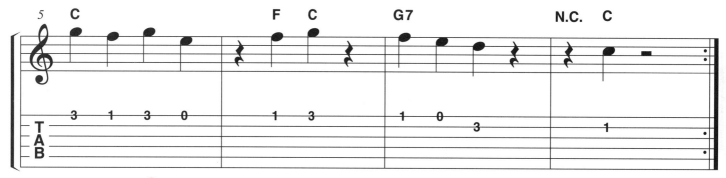

Bass Riff (59)

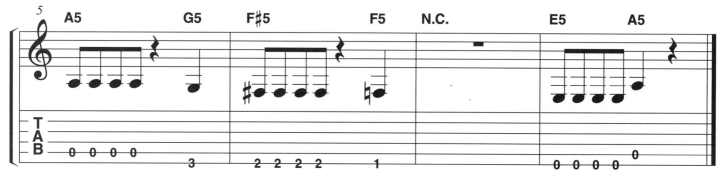

In "Bass Riff" use downstrokes to bring out the melody.

See the following excerpt of "Rocky Stones." Leave your first finger in place as you reach for the fourth fret with your third finger. You should be able to play each note without moving your left hand.

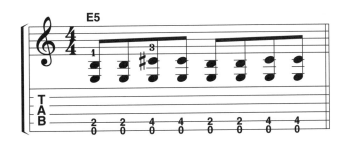

THE KEY OF C MAJOR

MAJOR SCALES

A **major scale** is a series of pitches arranged in ascending or descending order, beginning and ending with the same letter name. The distance between one letter name and the next is called a **step**. On the guitar, a **whole step** is two notes, two frets apart; a **half step** is two notes, one fret apart. The pattern of whole (W) and half (H) steps for a major scale is as follows:

W   W   H   W   W   W   H

Memorize the C major scale, ascending and descending. Notice that the scale extends for eight notes, one octave. Strive for a steady beat and evenness of tone.

The C Major Scale (memorize)

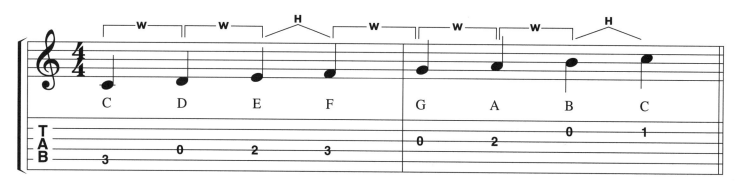

The pattern of whole steps and half steps is easily understood when playing a major scale on one string only, such as the C major scale on the second string.

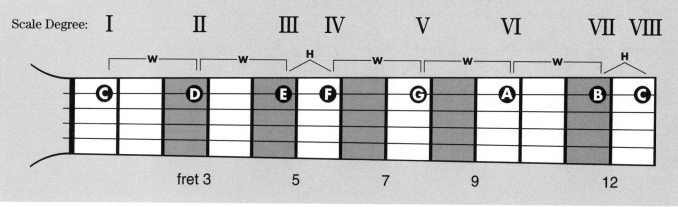

Try playing the major scale pattern (W W H W W W H) beginning on various strings and frets. For example, if you start with F on the first string (first fret), you would be playing an F major scale. With practice, you will develop the ability to recognize the sound of a major scale.

Songs using the notes of the C major scale are in the **Key of C**.
The Can Can is in the Key of C.

Jacques Offenbach

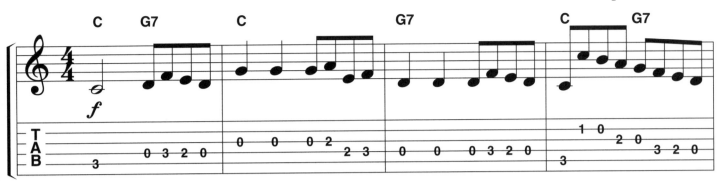

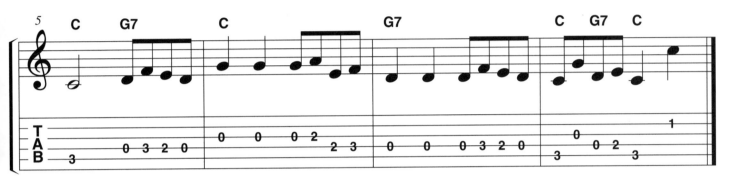

PRIMARY CHORDS

The **primary chords** of any key are based on the first (I), fourth (IV), and fifth (V) scale degrees. The primary chords in the Key of C are C, F, and G7.

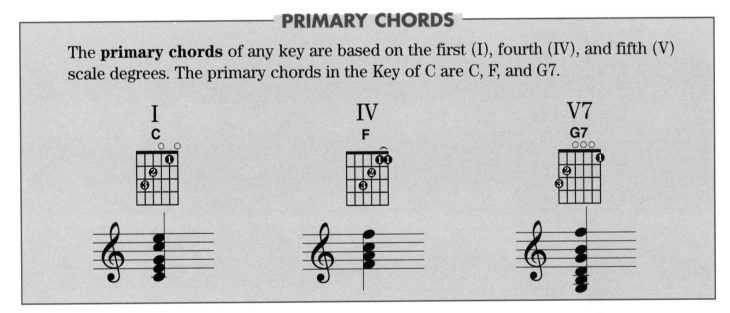

The F major chord uses a barre, and will become easier to play with practice. Be diligent! The F chord will prove to be very useful in the future, because it is movable. Practicing the F chord shape on higher frets (for example, barring the fifth fret) may be helpful.

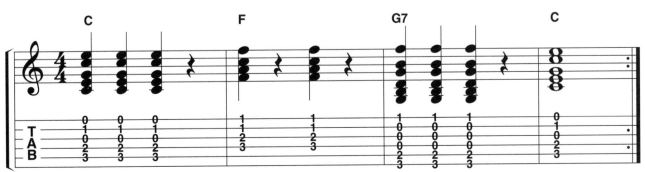

48

Texas Tornado 62

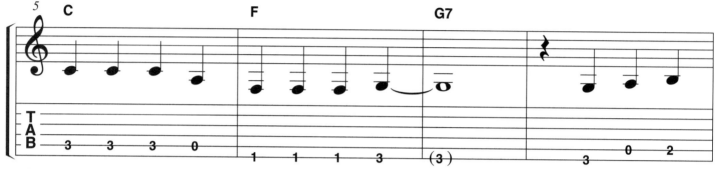

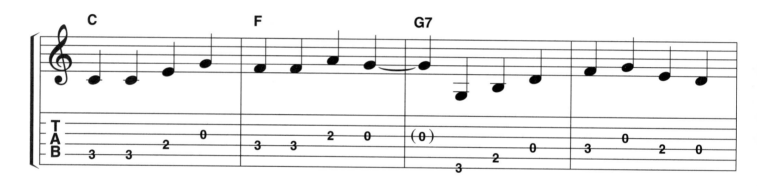

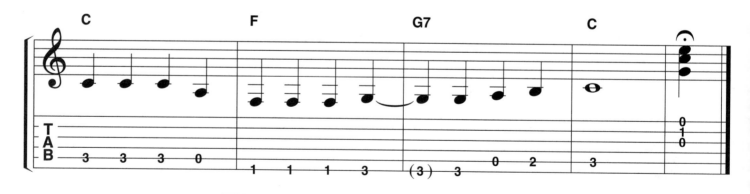

Whenever you learn a new key, as the Key of C (page 62), it is very important to memorize the major scale and be able to play it rapidly and confidently. You also must know the three primary chords (C, F, G7) and be able to play them easily and know how to move from chord to chord smoothly without hesitating.

G10

FLATS

A **flat** (♭) *lowers* the pitch of a note by one fret (one half step). The flat symbol stays in effect until the end of the measure. The chart below shows the location of flats, up to the fifth fret. Memorize the location of the open-string notes that are flat.

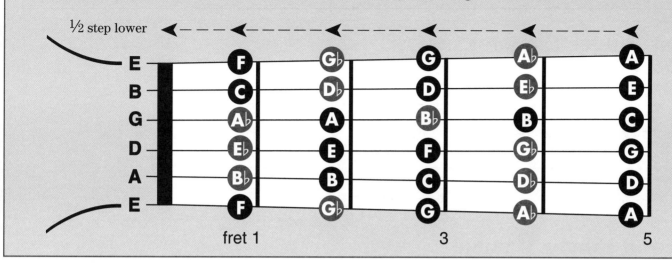

An open-string note with a flat needs to be played on the next lowest string.

Study in Flats

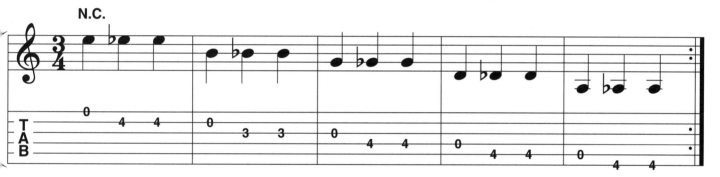

ENHARMONIC NOTES

Notes that have the same pitch, but different names, are called **enharmonic notes**.
One of the notes will be a sharp note; the other will be a flat note; for example, F♯ and G♭.
Write in the missing enharmonic notes.

D♯ and ____♭   ____♯ and D♭   A♯ and ____♭   ____♯ and A♭

(63) **Second-Place Blues**

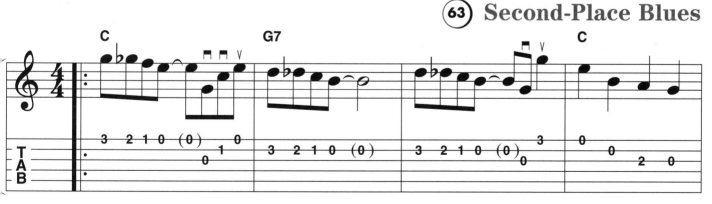

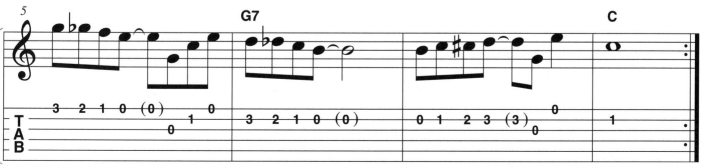

Two or more different notes may be connected by a curved line called a **slur**. When the second note is a higher pitch than the first, use a **hammer-on**. Play the first note with the pick, then the left-hand finger drops (like a hammer) to sound the second note. Keep a steady beat without rushing the slurred (second) note.

First Finger Hammer (64)

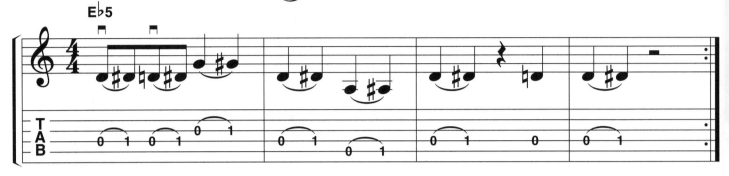

Second Finger Hammer

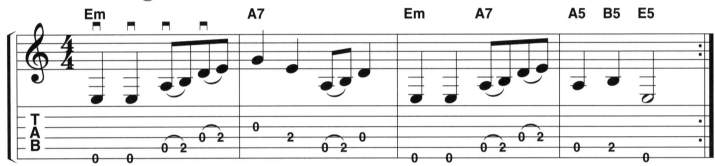

Third Finger Hammer

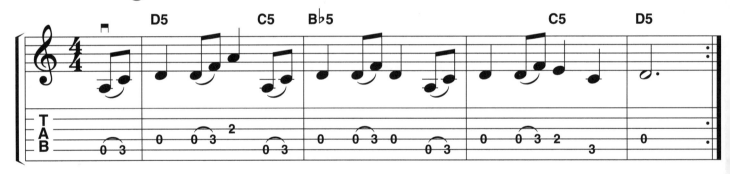

Hammerin' the Blues

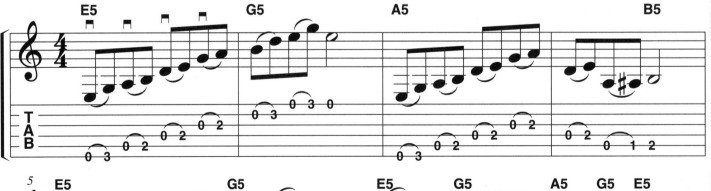

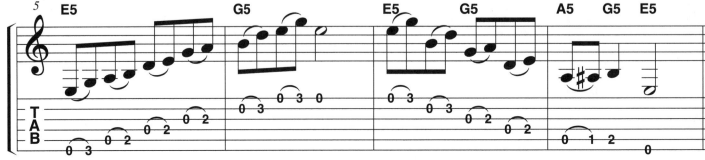

Fun Riffs

Sometimes it is fun to play short riffs instead of longer pieces of music. The following examples represent a variety of guitar music styles.

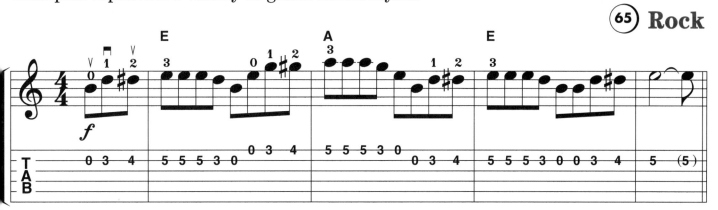

65) Rock

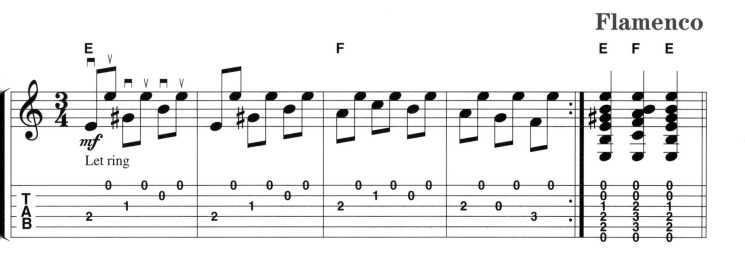

Flamenco

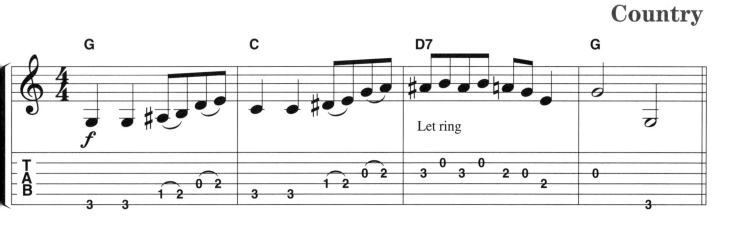

Country

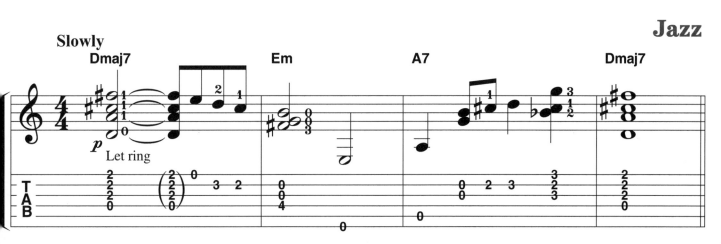

Jazz

The Star-Spangled Banner (66)

Francis Scott Key, John Stafford Smith

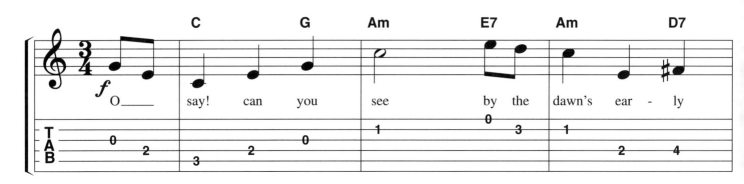

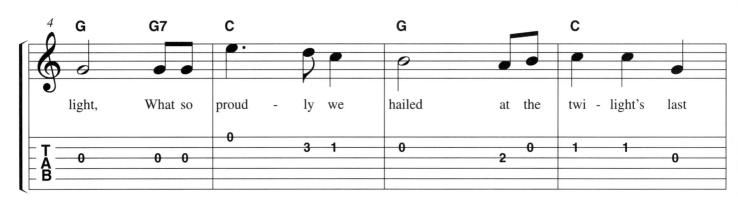

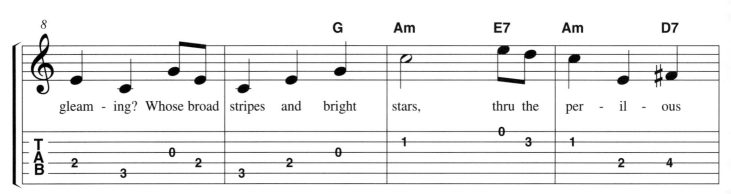

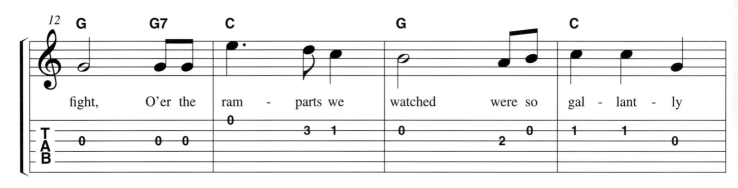

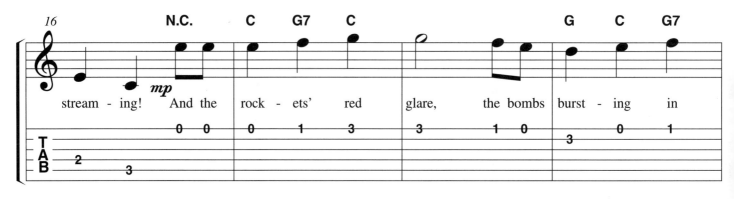

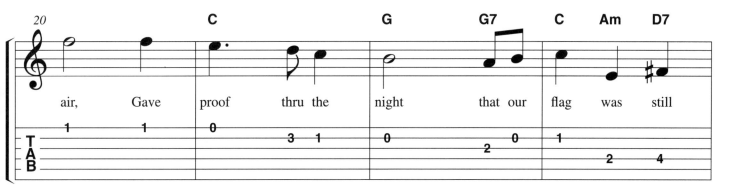

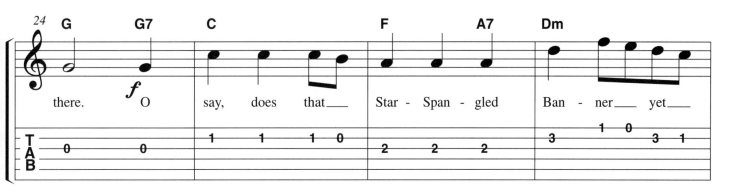

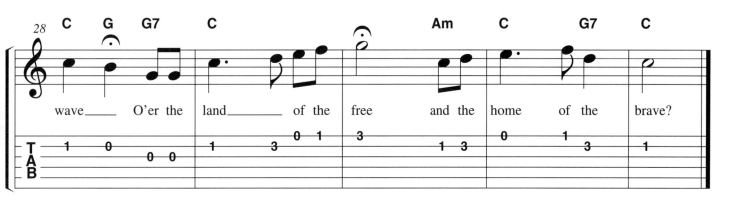

At this stage, hopefully you can play many of the songs in this book with the CD. This way you will be sure to easily advance through the last half of this book and have a lot of fun and satisfaction while doing it!

You have already acquired a lot of music knowledge by using this book. Increase your proficiency in reading music by playing as much music as you can. There are many supplemental guitar publications available to help you improve your music-reading skills without the use of tablature.

THE KEY OF G MAJOR

Let's review the pattern of whole (W) and half (H) steps used in major scales:

W   W   H   W   W   W   H

Play the G major scale on the third string only as shown below. Notice an F♯ is needed to keep the pattern of whole and half steps.

Scale Degree:

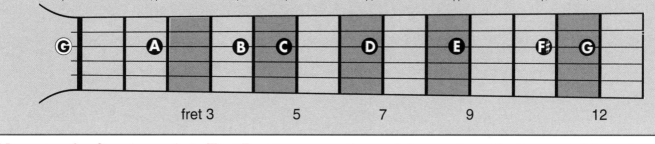

Memorize the G major scale in First Position, ascending and descending, playing smoothly and evenly.

The G Major Scale

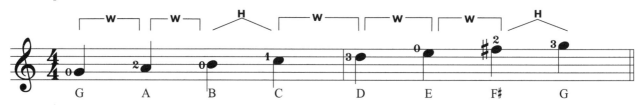

THE KEY SIGNATURE

 When playing music in the Key of G, all of the F's will be played sharp. Instead of writing sharps (♯) next to all F's in the music, we use a **key signature** on each line of music, placed directly after the treble clef. This indicates *all* F's are to be played sharp.

Songs using the notes of the G major scale are in the **Key of G**. Now play *The Can Can* in the Key of G.

The Can Can (67)

Jacques Offenbach

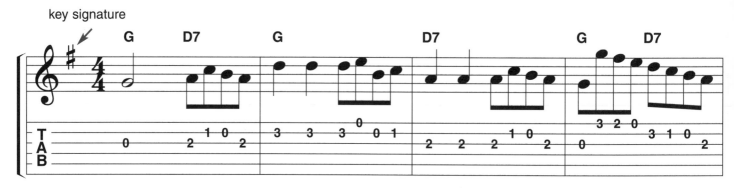

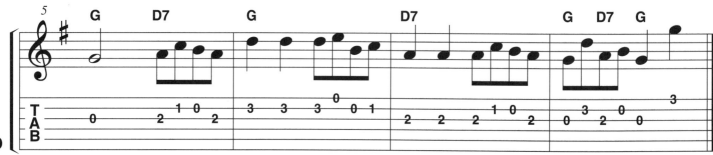

The primary chords in the Key of G are G (I), C (IV), and D7 (V7). The scale degrees are given the following names:

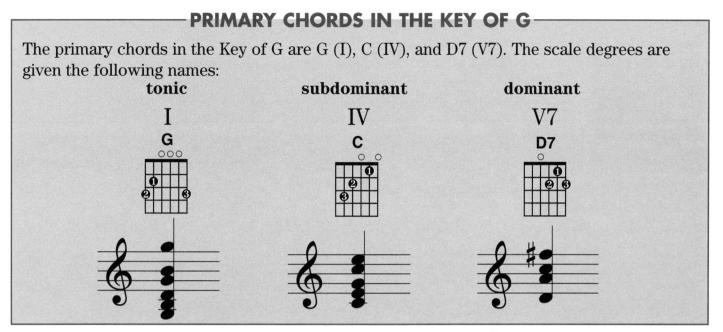

tonic   subdominant   dominant

I   IV   V7

G   C   D7

68 Joy to the World

Music by Lowell Mason

Joy to the world! The Lord is come; Let earth re-

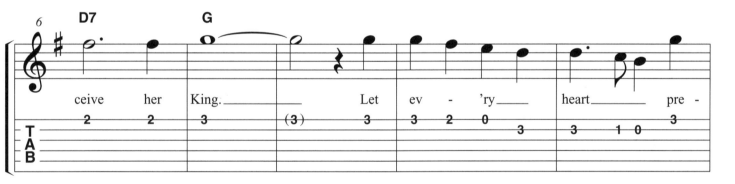

ceive her King. _____ Let ev-'ry_ heart_____ pre-

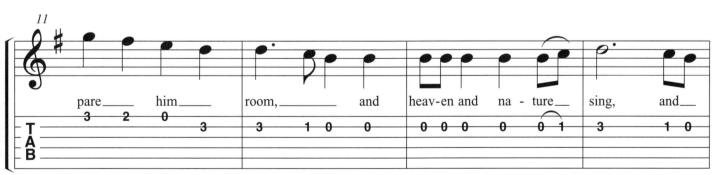

pare_ him_ room,_____ and heav-en and na-ture_ sing, and_

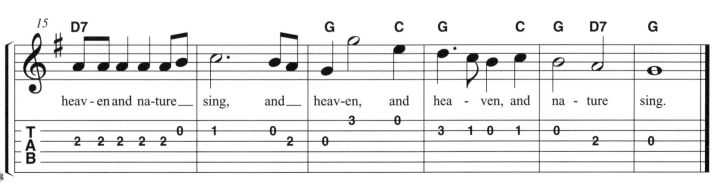

heav-en and na-ture_ sing, and_ heav-en, and hea-ven, and na-ture sing.

Minuet in G uses F♯'s on strings ①, ④, and ⑥ (indicated by arrows).
Remember that the key signature affects *all* F's on *all* strings.

Minuet in G 69

Christian Pezold

from the Notebook for Anna Magdalena Bach
by Johann Sebastian Bach

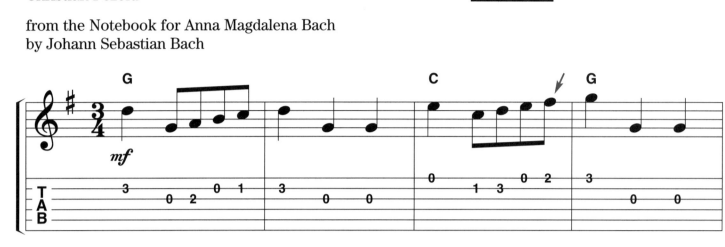

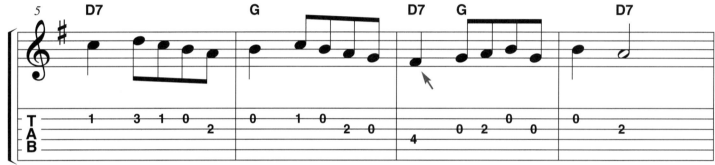

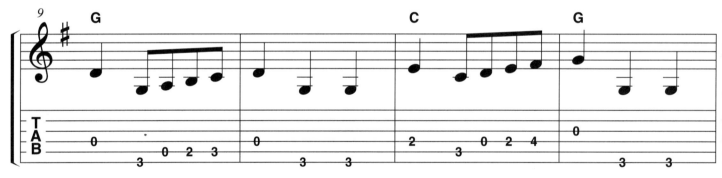

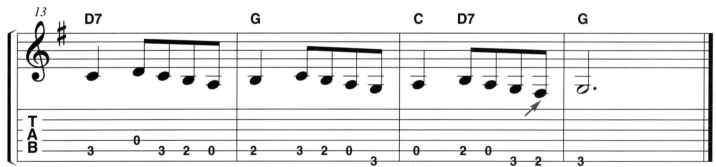

**Play a G scale in the lower octave. Start on G, sixth string, third fret.
Be sure to use the fourth finger for the F♯ on the fourth string.**

1ST AND 2ND ENDINGS

Play the first ending and take the repeat.
Then play the second ending, skipping over the first ending.

70 Berry B. Goode

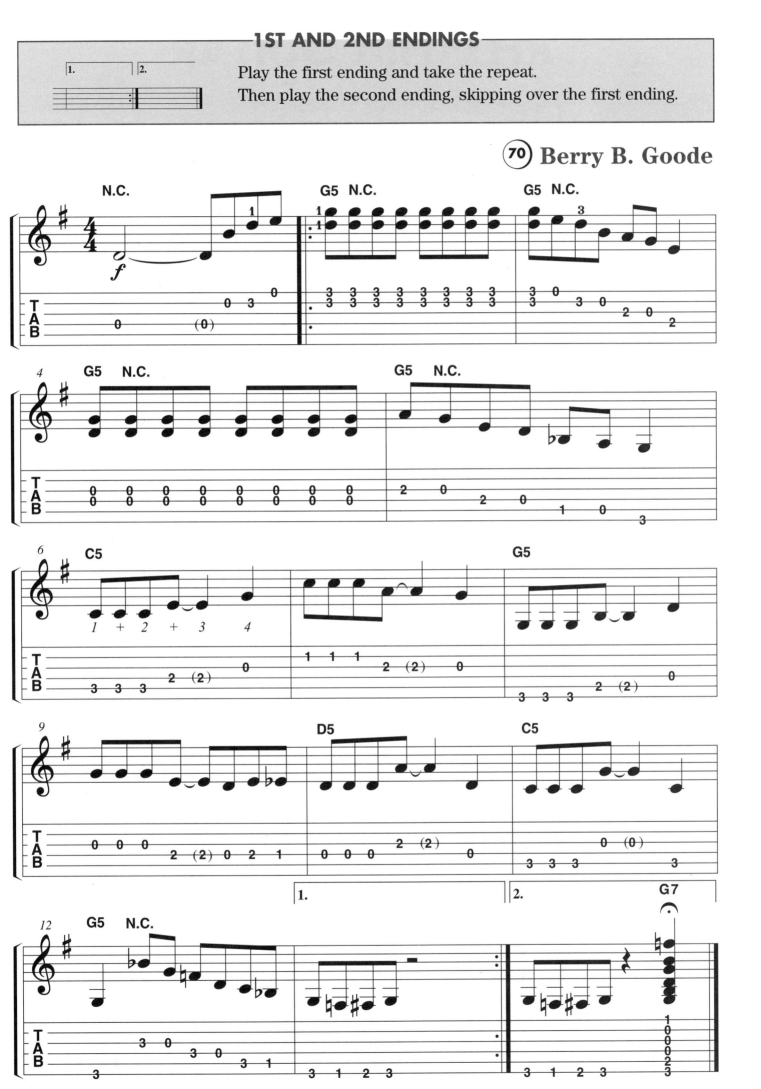

RHYTHM GUITAR

RIGHT-HAND STRUMMING

The guitar is an excellent instrument for providing chord accompaniment to many musical styles. Whether you are playing in a band or singing a folksong, the development of right-hand strumming skills will add depth and excitement to your playing.

 When playing the eighth-note strum pattern below, it is not necessary to play all of the strings on the upstroke (V). Let your ear be your guide. Use this strum for "He's Got the Whole World in His Hands."

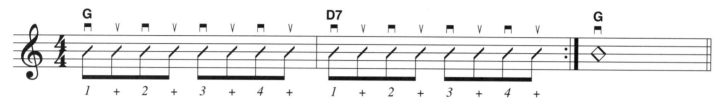

THE EIGHTH REST

The **eighth rest** gets ½ beat of silence. ⅄ = ½ beat
Be sure to dampen (mute) the strings to stop the sound during a rest.

He's Got the Whole World in His Hands 71

Traditional

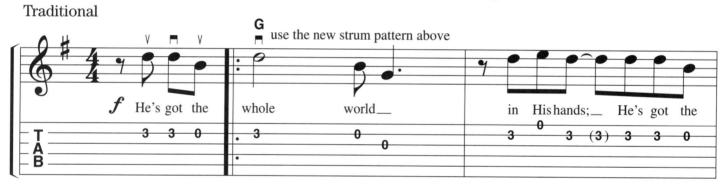

74

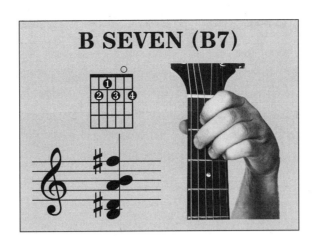

B SEVEN (B7)

New Strum Pattern

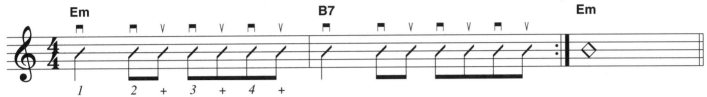

(72) # I've Been Working on the Railroad

American Folksong

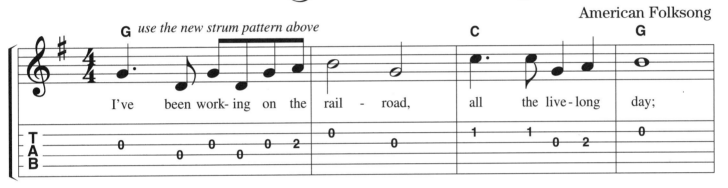

I've been work-ing on the rail - road, all the live-long day;

I've been work-ing on the rail - road, just to pass the time a - way.

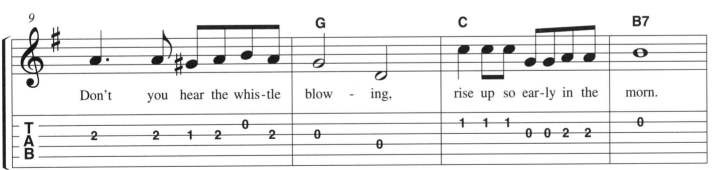

Don't you hear the whis-tle blow - ing, rise up so ear-ly in the morn.

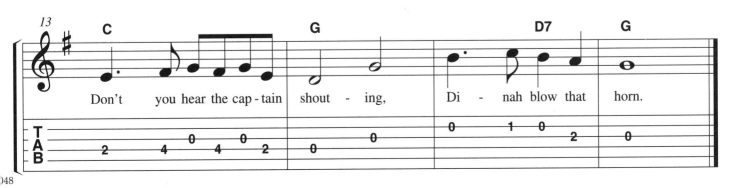

Don't you hear the cap-tain shout - ing, Di - nah blow that horn.

SYNCOPATED STRUMS

Syncopation is an accent on a weak beat. Syncopation may be used to create very interesting melodies and strum patterns. Practice the following three strum patterns as you count evenly. Keep your arm moving down-up-down-up smoothly, even when there are tied notes or rests in the melody. A strum pattern consists of hits and misses. The arm does not stop moving; it just misses the strings. Try out each of the strums below with *Bop, Sh' Bop*.

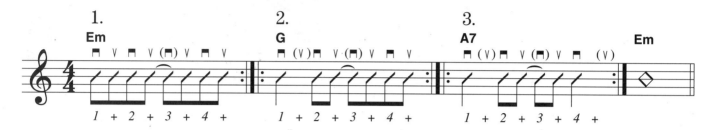

Bop, Sh' Bop (73)

76

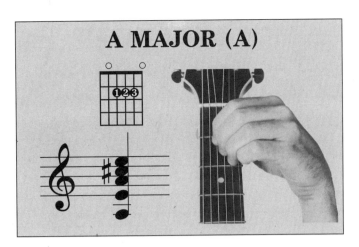

A MAJOR (A)

New Strum Pattern

(74) **The House of the Rising Sun**

American Folksong

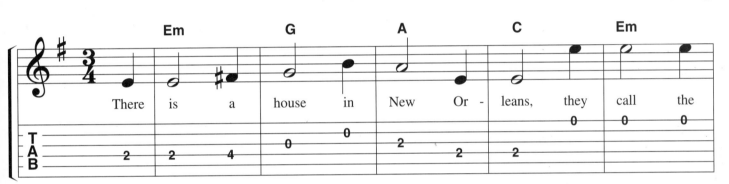

There is a house in New Or - leans, they call the

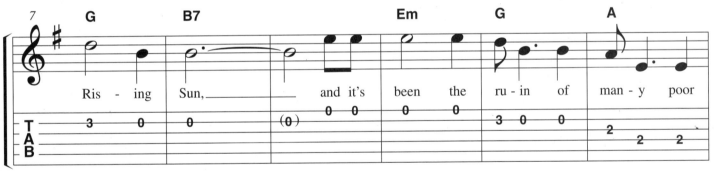

Ris - ing Sun,_____ and it's been the ru - in of man - y poor

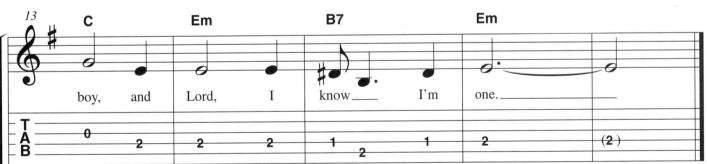

boy, and Lord, I know____ I'm one._____

Use an alternate fingering for the G chord to make use of a common finger.

There are several acceptable left-hand fingerings for the A chord. Use common fingers as much as possible.

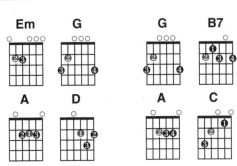

EIGHTH-NOTE TRIPLETS

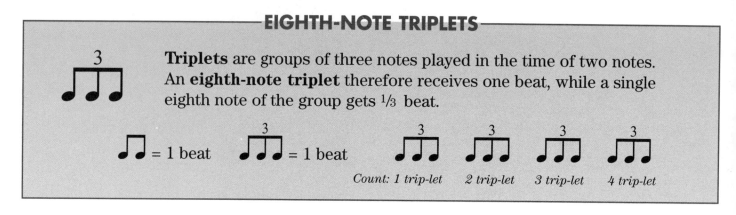

Triplets are groups of three notes played in the time of two notes. An **eighth-note triplet** therefore receives one beat, while a single eighth note of the group gets ⅓ beat.

♪♪ = 1 beat   ♪♪♪ = 1 beat

Count: 1 trip-let   2 trip-let   3 trip-let   4 trip-let

Studies Using Eighth-Note Triplets

Familiar Melodies Using Eighth-Note Triplets

March from *The Nutcracker Suite* by Peter Ilyich Tchaikovsky

75

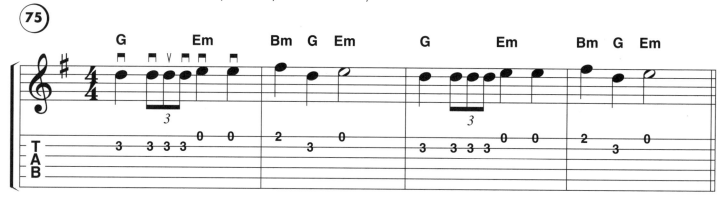

A Classic Blues ending

78

76 Jesu, Joy of Man's Desiring

Johann Sebastian Bach

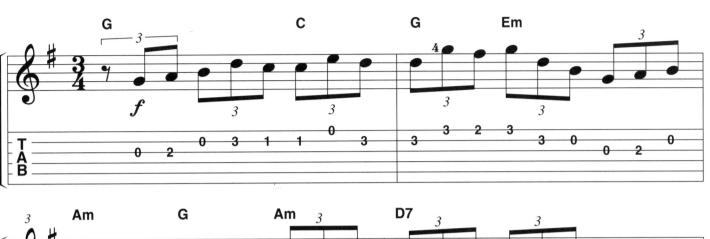

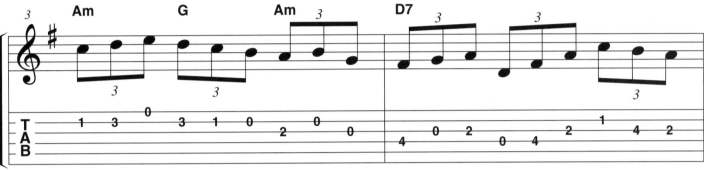

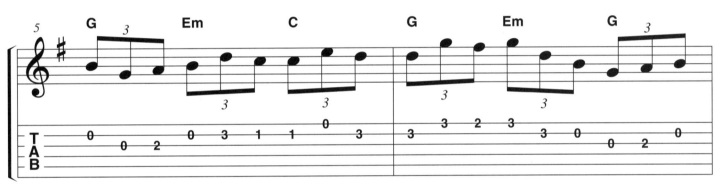

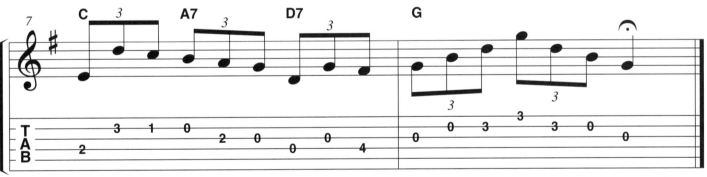

Even though the first triplet group in measure 1 starts with a rest, count the figure the same way as before (1 trip-let).

***Jesu, Joy of Man's Desiring** is in the key of _____ .*

In addition to recognizing the key signature, look at the first and last chord names. They will usually identify the key as well.

SWING RHYTHM

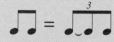

Swing rhythm (sometimes referred to as a **shuffle**), is a musical style that uses an uneven eighth-note rhythm with long and short values. Based on triplets by tying the first two notes of the group, swing gives the melody a pleasing jazz sound. The downbeats (beats 1, 2, 3, and 4) will always be long; the upbeats (the "and" or "+" of the beat) will always be short. Swing rhythm is indicated at the beginning of the music.

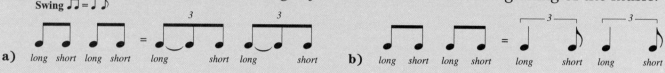

Charlie's Swing ⑦

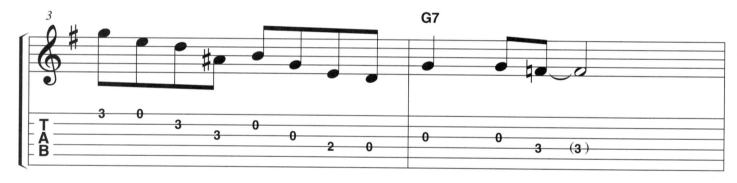

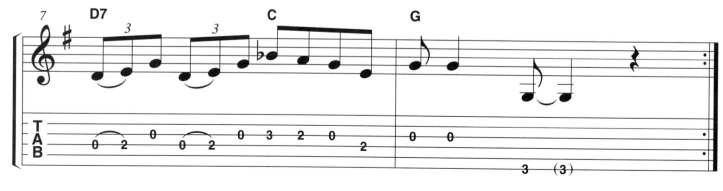

80

G10

With swing rhythm, the last eighth note of a measure leads directly into the first beat of the next measure. Exaggerate the long-short rhythms for the best effect.

Swing was a big band jazz style, very popular in the 1930s and 1940s. Learning how to "feel" swing is an important musical concept. Play along with the CD until you can match the rhythm easily.

MOVING UP THE FINGERBOARD

The fingerboard chart below shows the natural notes you have learned up to the fifth fret (black notes). It also shows other places to find these notes (red notes).

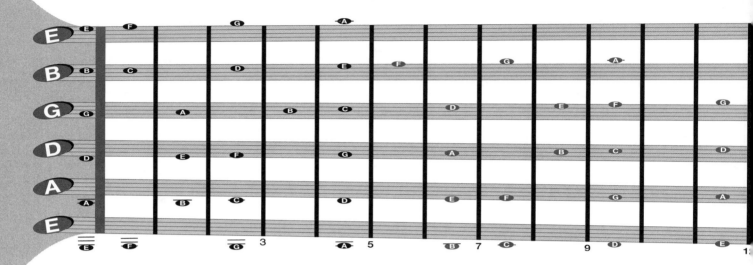

Play the pitches of third string G - A, first on the fourth, and then the fifth strings.
Play the pitches of fourth string D - E, first on the fifth, and then the sixth strings.
Play the pitches of fifth string A - B - C on the sixth string.

CHANGING POSITIONS

A **position** on the guitar consists of four adjacent frets. For example, First Position uses frets 1, 2, 3, and 4; Fifth Position uses frets 5, 6, 7, and 8; and Ninth Position use frets 9, 10, 11, and 12. The position is named for the *lowest-numbered* fret, which is played with the first finger.

Now play *Study in Quarter Notes* from page 8 in First Position, Fifth Position, and Ninth Position. Use the chart above to help you. **When reading the tablature, be sure to play only one string at a time!**

Study in Quarter Notes *(play only one string at a time)*

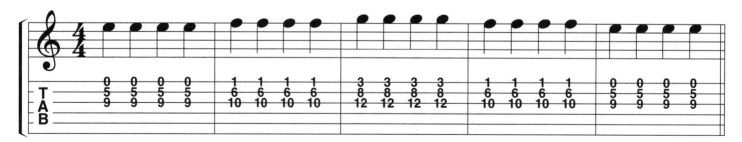

Notice that each string has a characteristic sound, even when playing the same pitches. The more you become acquainted with these new notes, the more you may decide to play certain notes on different strings.

MOVABLE POWER CHORDS

Many pop, rock, and blues songs use **movable power chords**. The power chord shape may be moved up or down the neck. Both fingers may be used as guide fingers. Refer to the chart on page 82.

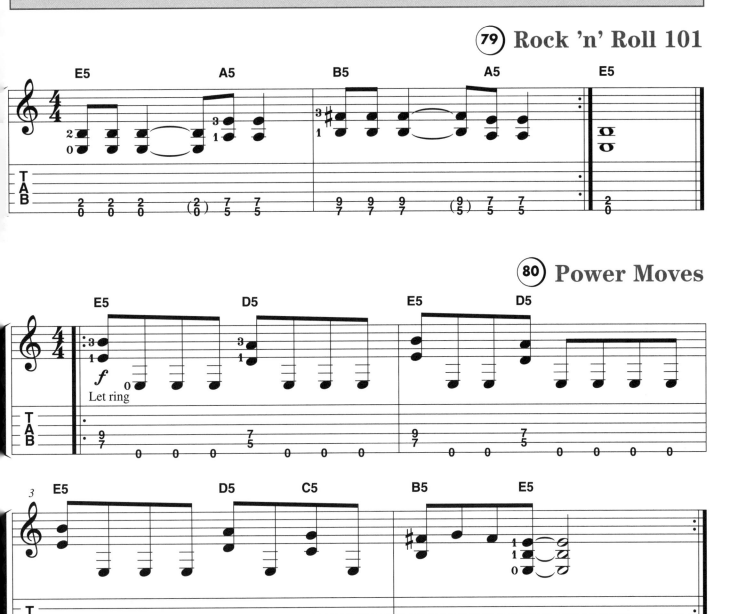

79 Rock 'n' Roll 101

80 Power Moves

PALM MUTE

To play a **palm mute** (notated PM), let the side of your right-hand palm lightly rest on the strings near the bridge. Listen to the CD for the desired sound. The **palm mute** is very effective on bass-string solos or with power chords.

BLUES SESSION

RIFFS

A **riff** is a short, melodic fragment that can be used as a repetitive pattern in a song when improvising a lead solo. The following blues riff is used by guitar players and bass players alike. Its many variations are often used in popular music.

Play this riff on E in **Fifth Position:**

first finger	*plays on the*	fifth fret
second finger	*plays on the*	sixth fret
third finger	*plays on the*	seventh fret
fourth finger	*plays on the*	eighth fret

Use the tablature as a guide.

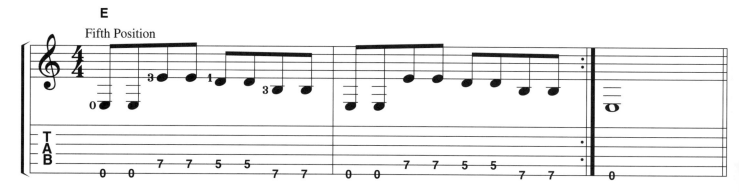

 Begin practicing using straight eighth notes. When the notes and rhythm are very accurate, play the riff using swing rhythm. Both straight eighth notes and swing rhythm work equally well with this riff.

Now play the same pattern beginning with the fifth string open A.

Riffin' (81)

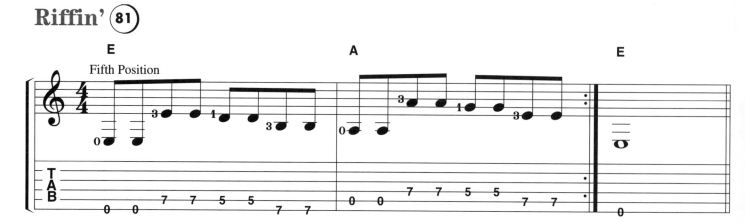

84

Using the "A" riff learned on the previous page, start with the note "A" on the sixth string at the fifth fret. Every other note is played in the same place as before.

Now that there are no open strings, the pattern can be moved around to different frets. For example, the blues riff on G is played in Third Position.

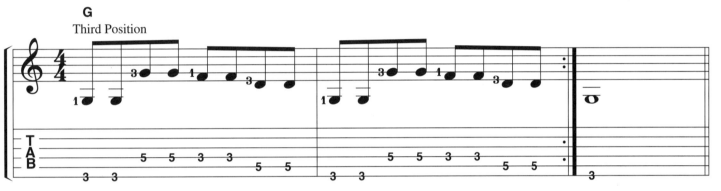

Now play the blues riff starting on B in Seventh Position.

This riff may also begin on the fifth string, as shown below on the C riff. Remember that the first finger always starts this riff.

Play the blues riff on other frets up and down the fingerboard. The riff will be named after the starting note. Be sure that you can name each starting note. Review the fingerboard chart on page 82.

12-BAR BLUES

The **12-Bar Blues Progression** has been the basis for numerous pop, rock, and blues songs. The progression uses the primary chords (I, IV, and V7) from a given key. Up to this point you have learned the primary chords in the Key of C (C, F, and G7) and the Key of G (G, C, and D7).

The Key of E is often used in the blues, and will therefore be a great starting point in learning the 12-Bar Blues.

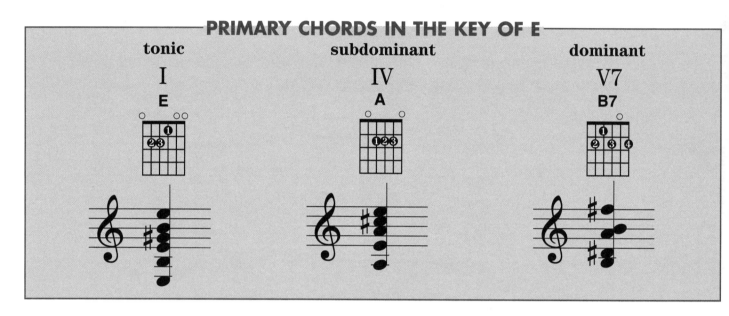

Using the Roman numerals as a guide, strum chords to *The 12-Bar Blues Progression* in the Key of E. Use a strum from page 12 or create your own.

The 12-Bar Blues Progression (82)

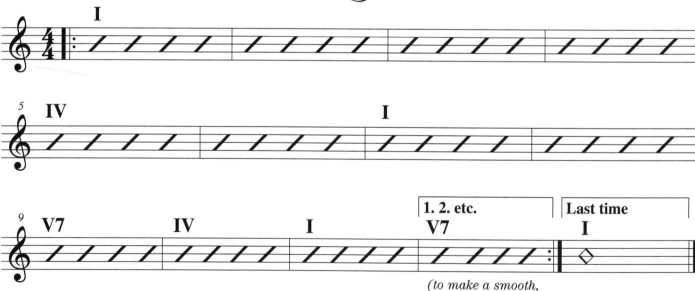

(to make a smooth, interesting repeat)

Can you strum chords to the *12-Bar Blues Progression* in the Key of G? In the Key of C?

I	IV	V7
G	C	D7
C	F	G7

Everybody's Blues uses the blues riff pattern learned on pages 84 and 85 as well as the *12-Bar Blues Progression* on page 24. Practice along with your teacher, a friend, or the CD, switching parts on the repeat. Memorize the chord progression.

(83) **Everybody's Blues**

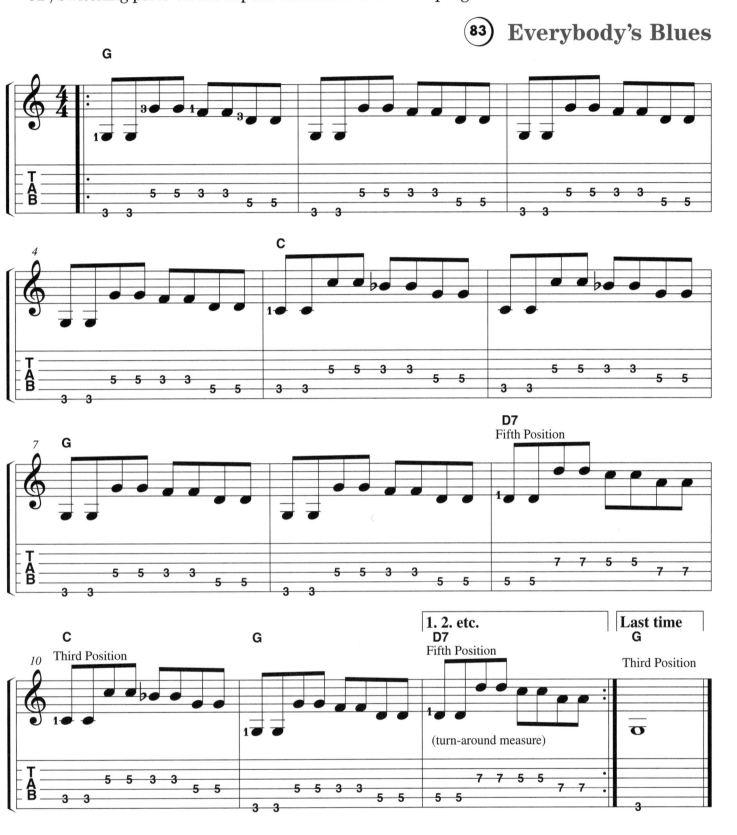

Can you play the lead guitar riff and the chords to *Everybody's Blues* in the Key of C?

I	IV	V7
C	F	G7

Lead Guitar Tip: The starting note for the IV chord may be a higher *or* lower pitch than the starting note for the I chord. Play C on the fifth string, and the F and G on the sixth string.

THE KEY OF A MINOR

RELATIVE MINOR

Every major key has a **relative minor** key. The relative minor key uses identical notes to the major key, and begins on the sixth degree of the major scale. The relative minor key to C major is A minor.

Unlike major keys, minor keys have three different types of scales: Natural Minor, Harmonic Minor, and Melodic Minor. We will study the natural and harmonic scales in this book.
Memorize the A minor scales, ascending and descending.
Play *legato*, and strive for a steady beat and evenness of tone.
(W = Whole step, H = Half step, 1½ = one and a half steps)

A Natural Minor

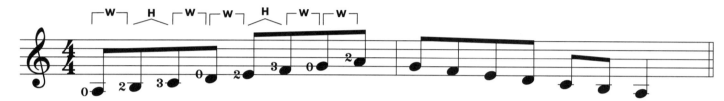

A Harmonic Minor (raise the seventh degree by one half step)

Now play *The Can Can* in the Key of A minor, using the A harmonic minor scale. Notice a *very* different mood created by the use of a minor key.

The Can Can (84)
Jacques Offenbach

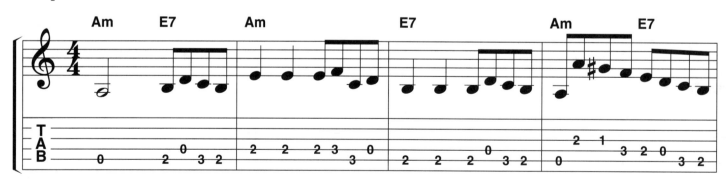

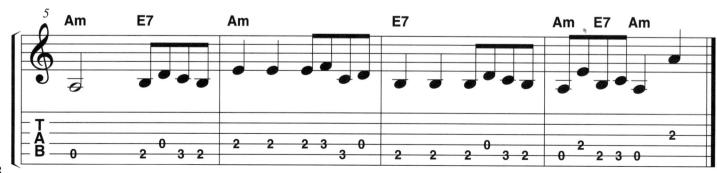

G

PRIMARY CHORDS IN THE KEY OF A MINOR

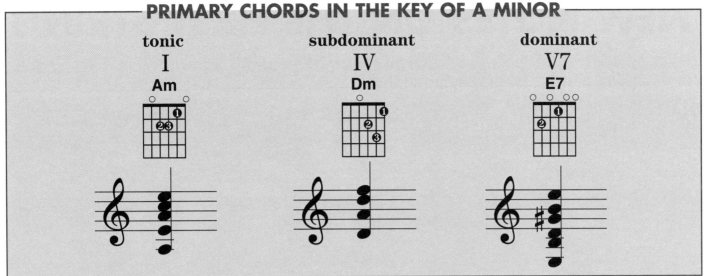

tonic	subdominant	dominant
I	IV	V7
Am	Dm	E7

Django Reinhardt (1910–1954) was an outstanding jazz guitarist who played in the famous Hot Club of France. His gypsy-influenced music was very popular in Europe in his day, and is now an influence on jazz guitarists throughout the world.

85 Django's Swing

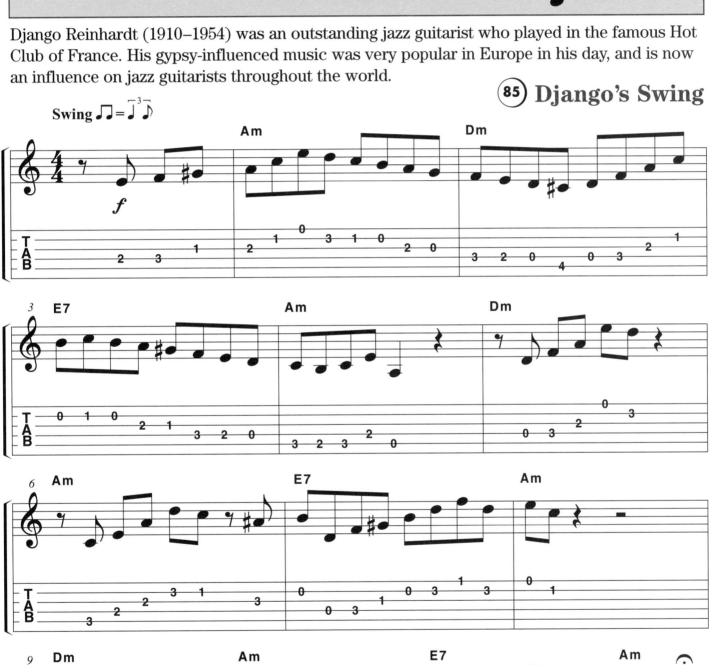

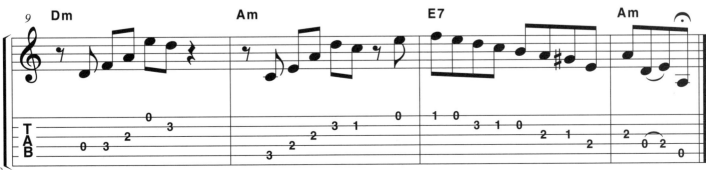

NEW NOTES ON THE FIRST STRING

Below are the natural notes on the first string up to the twelfth fret. Ledger lines are needed for the higher pitches written above the staff.

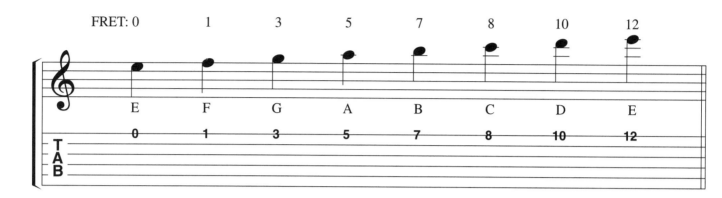

Memorize the name and location of all natural notes on the first string. Be able to play the notes at random while saying (or singing) the note names aloud. Do the same thing with the sharp and flat notes on the first string.

Octave Challenge
The following octave study is a very useful pattern to aid you in remembering the location of the new first-string notes. Keep your first and fourth left-hand fingers ready to change positions as the pattern goes up the fingerboard.

Fretboard Challenge
Fill in the missing note names on the fingerboard chart below.

The notes on the 12th fret are one octave higher than the open-string notes.

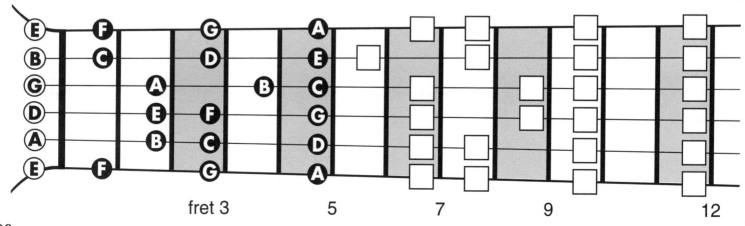

G1

THE PULL-OFF

A **pull-off** is a slur in which the second note is a *lower* pitch than the first (the opposite of a hammer-on). Play the first note with your right hand, then *pull* your left-hand finger *off* (toward the floor) to sound the second note.

Pull-off Warm-up

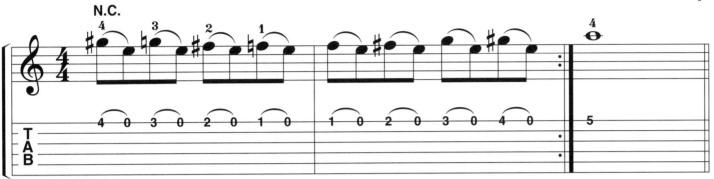

(86) Fantasia on the First String

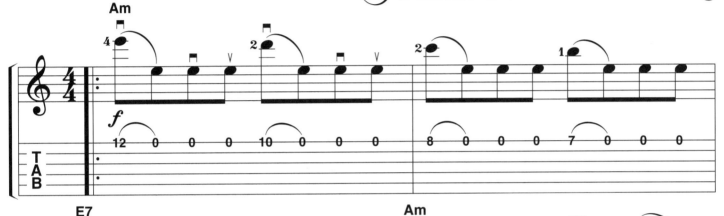

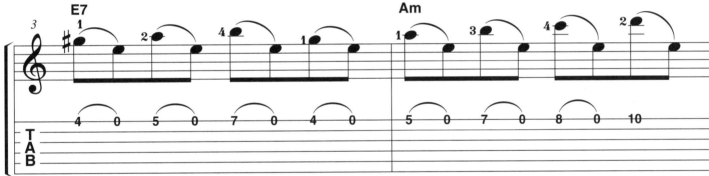

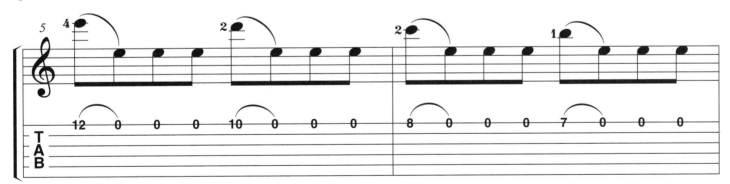

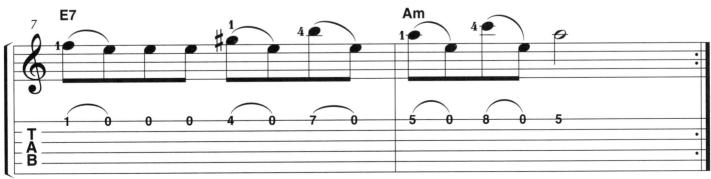

FIFTH POSITION
Natural Note Fingerboard Chart

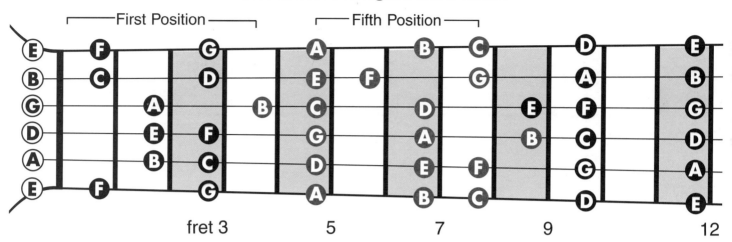

 In order to play the natural notes in Fifth Position, it is necessary to use a **position extension**. The B may be played on the third string at the fourth fret or on the fourth string at the ninth fret (see the chart above).

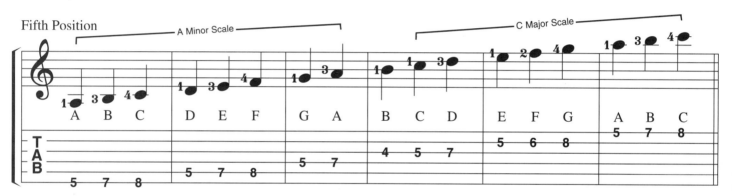

Memorize both the A minor and C major scales in Fifth Position.

We Three Kings (87)

J.H. Hopkins, Jr.

Fifth Position

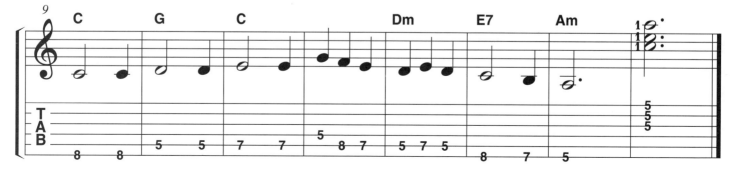

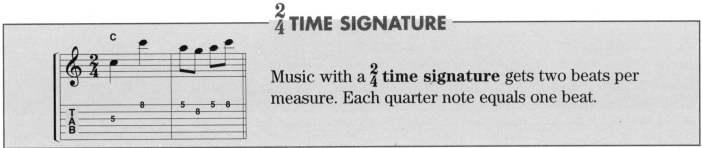

$\frac{2}{4}$ TIME SIGNATURE

Music with a $\frac{2}{4}$ time **signature** gets two beats per measure. Each quarter note equals one beat.

(88) # Miss McLeod's Reel

Scottish Traditional

The melody for *Miss McLeod's Reel* includes the notes of the C major scale as indicated on page 92.

Miss McLeod's Reel uses the __ __ __ __ __ __ __ Chords in the Key of C.
Hint: I, IV, and V7

PENTATONIC SCALE

The **pentatonic scale** is the basis for lead guitar solos in many pop, rock, country, and blues songs. It is made up of five different notes, as opposed to seven found in major or minor scales. There will generally be only two notes played on each string. The pentatonic scale may be major or minor.

- The pentatonic scale below is the most common scale used for rock soloing. The same pattern can be used for *both* the major and minor pentatonic scales.
- The root (or key note) of each scale is shown in color.
- Because there are no open strings, the pattern is movable.

C Major Pentatonic

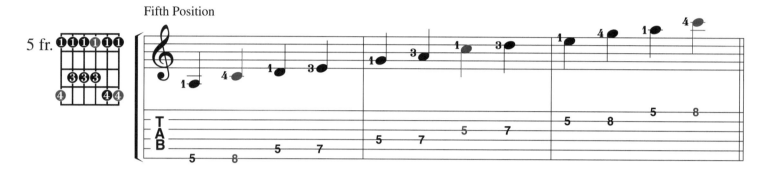

San Souci (89)
(without cares)

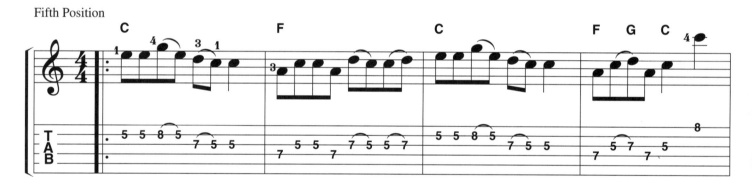

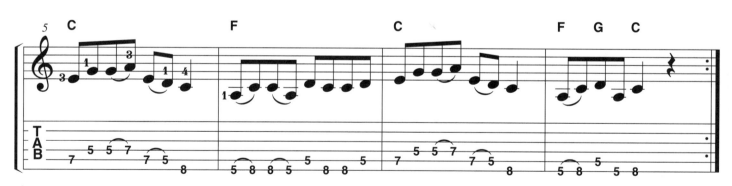

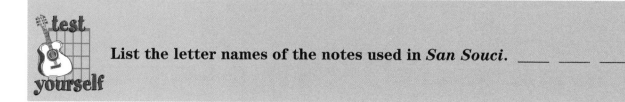

List the letter names of the notes used in *San Souci*. ____ ____ ____ ____ ____

A Minor Pentatonic

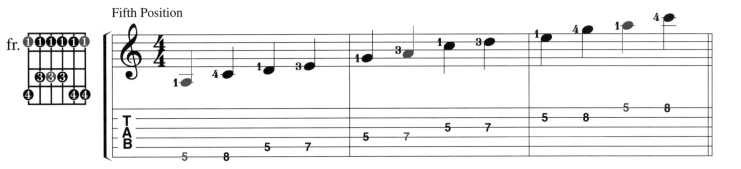

Fifth Position

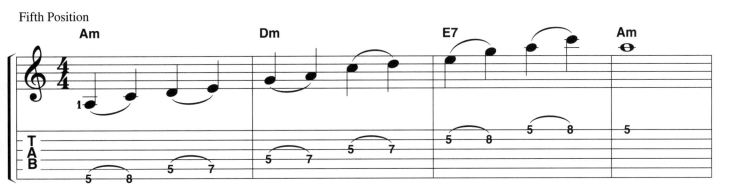

(90) **Rock Scaling**

Fifth Position

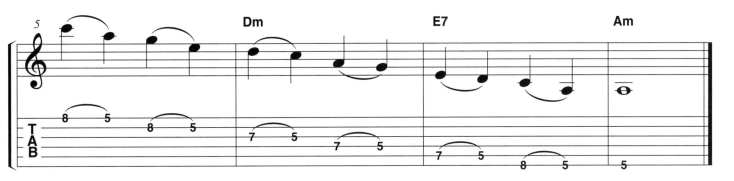

Say the note names aloud as you play *Rock Scaling*.

To help you decide if a song is in a major key or a minor key look at the first and last chord names. The key will most likely be the same as these two chords.

The minor pentatonic scale has been used more than any other scale for popular guitar solos. Memorize this scale to create your own riffs and solos. Analyze how the minor pentatonic scale is used in "Friends of Mine" on pages 96-97. "Hammerin' the Blues" on page 66 is a good example of E minor pentatonic using the open strings.

Friends of Mine ⑨¹

STUDENT DUET

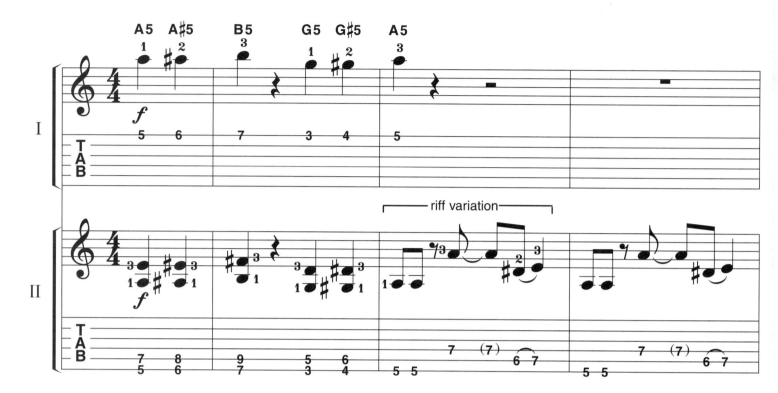

 "Friends of Mine" uses several popular guitar techniques you have already learned.

- *Power Chords*
- *A variation of the blues riff learned on page 84*
- *The minor pentatonic scale*
- *Playing in positions other than First Position*

Be sure that you have command of these four widely used techniques.

G1

BOOGIE RIFF

The **boogie riff** is similar in usage to the blues riff on page 84. It has many variations that are often used in popular music. **Be sure to practice this riff in various positions up and down the fretboard!**

The boogie riff is used below in a **6-Bar Blues Progression.** (I = A; IV = D; V7 = E7) Use the tablature as a guide.

Begin playing this riff on A in **Fourth Position:**

first finger	*plays on the*	fourth fret
second finger	*plays on the*	fifth fret
third finger	*plays on the*	sixth fret
fourth finger	*plays on the*	seventh fret

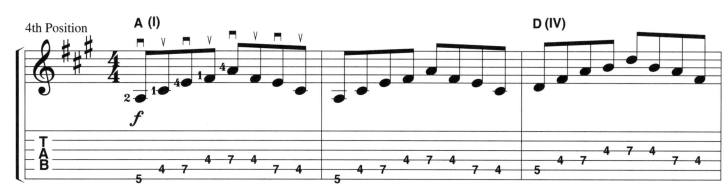

Variations of the boogie riff

MUSICIANSHIP
(The Art of Playing Music Expressively)

One of the most important (if not the most rewarding) aspects of becoming a musician is learning how to play music with expression. Once you have learned the correct notes and rhythm to a piece of music, you should then work on making the music sound beautiful.

EXPRESSION MARKS

To add expression to your music you may use variations of **articulation**, **dynamics**, **tempo**, **timbre** (TAM-bur), and **vibrato**. Some music will already have suggested expression marks. Exaggerate these techniques for best results.

Articulation – (accents)

legato = smooth *staccato* = detached *marcato* = marked

Dynamics – (volume)

pp	*pianissimo*	very soft	*mf*	*mezzo forte*	moderately loud
p	*piano*	soft	*f*	*forte*	loud
mp	*mezzo piano*	moderately soft	*ff*	*fortissimo*	very loud
	crescendo	becoming louder		*diminuendo*	becoming softer

Tempo – (speed)

Adagio	slow		**Moderato**	moderate
Andante	a slow walking tempo		**Allegro**	a fast, cheerful tempo
ritard.	becoming slower		*accel.*	becoming faster

Timbre – (tone color)

ponticello = play the string near the bridge to produce a very bright or brittle sound
dolce = play the string near the fingerboard to produce a sweet sound

Vibrato – Guitarists will often fluctuate (or vibrate) the pitch of a note with the left hand. It is usually accomplished by quickly moving the left-hand finger back and forth while fingering a note.

⑨③ In the Hall of the Mountain King

Edvard Grieg

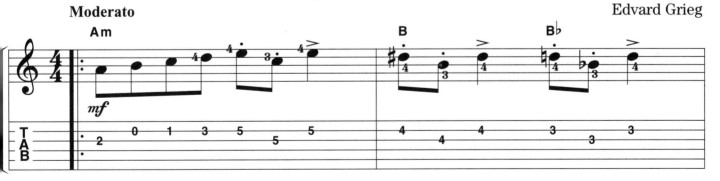

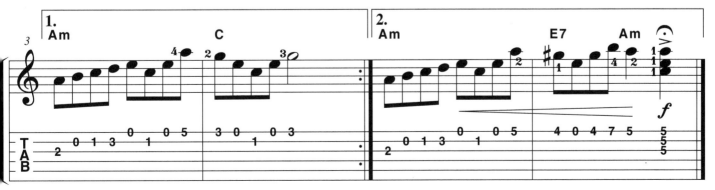

99

FINGERSTYLE

The right-hand thumb and fingers are often used to sound the strings. Each finger has a letter name derived from the Spanish word.

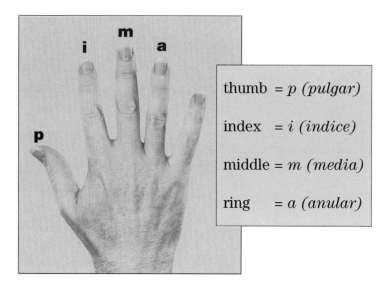

thumb = *p (pulgar)*

index = *i (indice)*

middle = *m (media)*

ring = *a (anular)*

Right-Hand Positioning

- Position your right hand towards the midpoint between the bridge and the fingerboard, or the edge of the soundhole.

- The wrist should be aligned naturally with the hand and forearm.

- The fingers (*i*, *m*, and *a*) should be held in a relaxed curve, as if you are holding a bubble.

- The thumb (*p*) is extended slightly, allowing the thumb and fingers to play without bumping into each other.

- The nails may be used to help produce a louder and more beautiful sound. File your nails so that they pass smoothly over the strings.

THE FREE STROKE

When using the free stroke, the right-hand finger does not touch or rest on any other string.

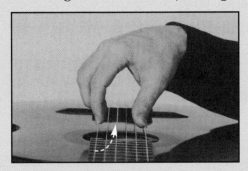

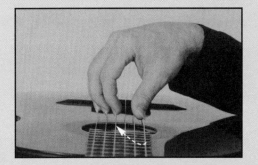

- Place (or prepare) the fingertip on the string.

- Play the string with a "scratching" motion, moving mostly from the knuckle.

- When playing free strokes, your finger will pass *freely* over the adjacent string.

- Place or prepare the thumb on the string.

- Play the string with a forward and upward motion.

- Your thumb will pass *freely* over the adjacent string.

(94) Fingerstyle Blues

101

Some of the most beautiful songs ever written use **fingerstyle accompaniment patterns:**
Stairway to Heaven, Led Zeppelin; *Time in a Bottle*, Jim Croce; *Fire and Rain*, James
Taylor; *The Sound of Silence*, Simon and Garfunkel; *Blackbird*, The Beatles; *Dust in the
Wind*, Kansas; and many more.

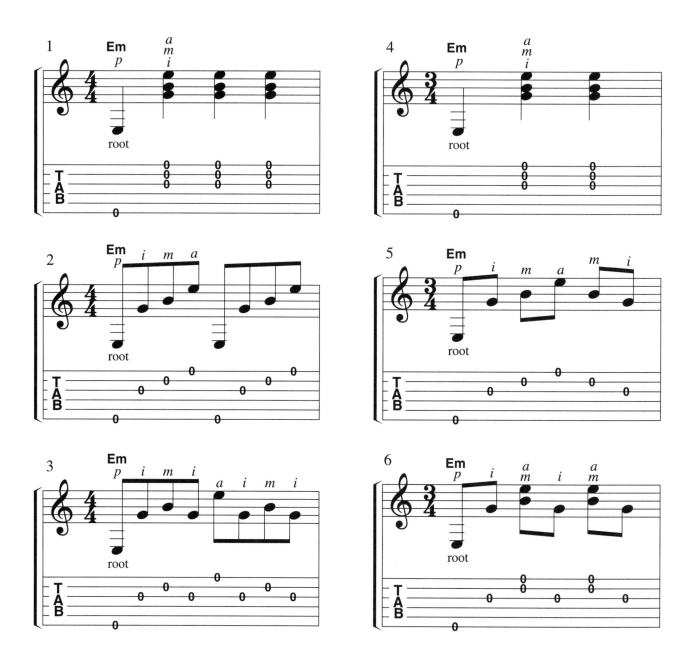

*When playing two or three notes together with the right-hand fingers,
move the fingers together as if they were one large finger. Practice the
accompaniment patterns every day, striving for smoothness and
evenness in sound and rhythm. Let all notes ring.*

English Folksong

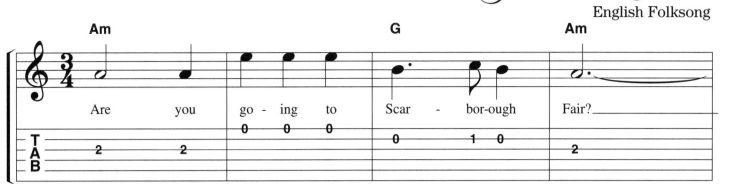

Are you go - ing to Scar - bor-ough Fair?

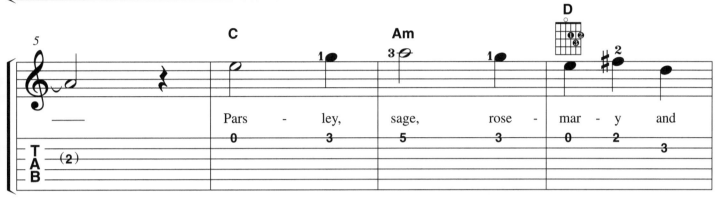

Pars - ley, sage, rose - mar - y and

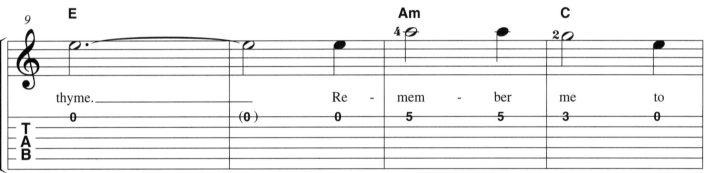

thyme. Re - mem - ber me to

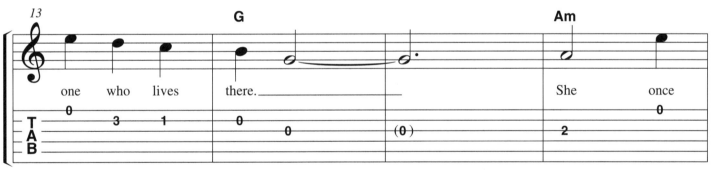

one who lives there. She once

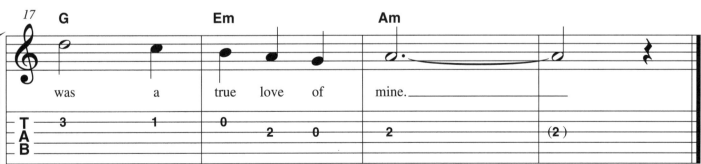

was a true love of mine.

Use fingerstyle pattern No. 5 from page 102 when playing the accompaniment to "Scarborough Fair."

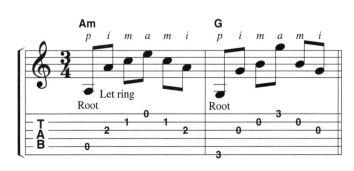

103

Malagueña

Spanish

Malagueña uses a specialized F chord. The chord name approximates the harmony.

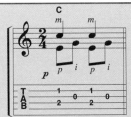

Andantino has a melody (using upstems) and an accompaniment (using downstems) that are played at the same time. This use of double stemming is also referred to as playing two voices.

(97) Andantino

Matteo Carcassi (arranged)

D.C. al Fine - *Go back to the beginning of the piece and end at the* ***Fine*** *(FEE-nay). D.C. al Fine is an abbreviation for Da Capo al Fine, which means "from the beginning to the end."*

Take Me Out to the Ball Game (98)

Jack Norworth and Albert von Tilzer

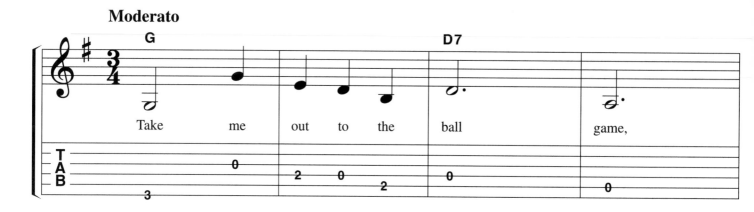

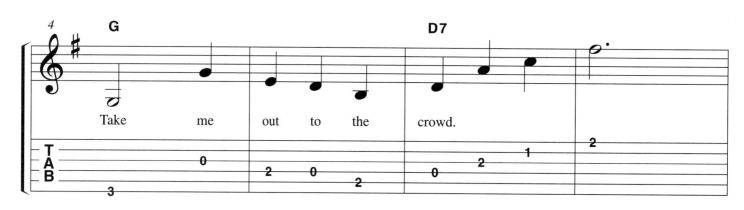

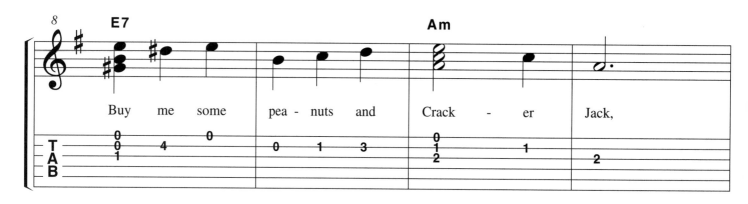

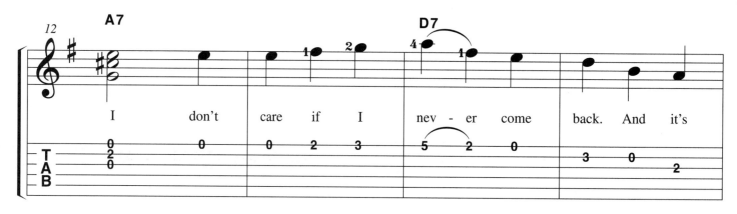

Congratulations, you have successfully completed **Everybody's Guitar Tablature Method.** Be sure that you can play every song in this book with ease. Can you play each song along with the CD?

048

107

Country Rock 99

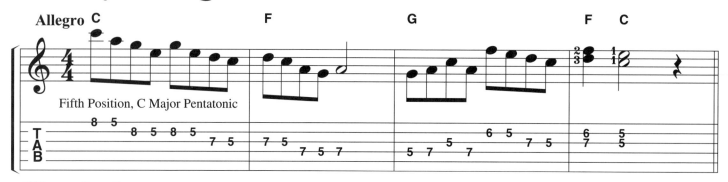

Classical (*Lagrìma*)

Francisco Tárrega

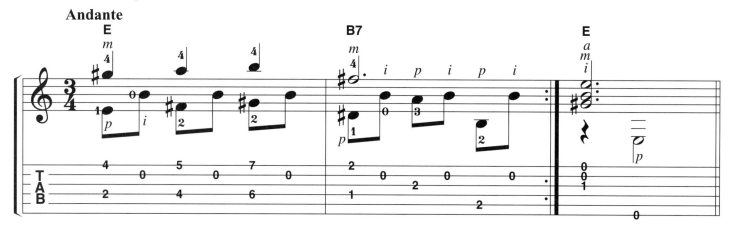

Popular (fingerstyle)

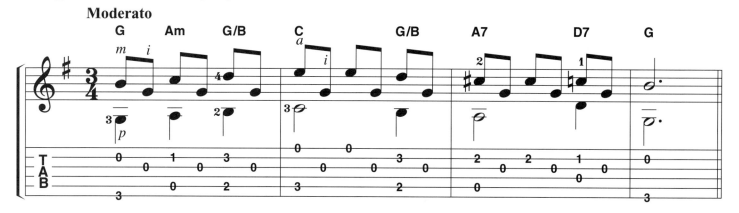

Blues (fingerstyle)

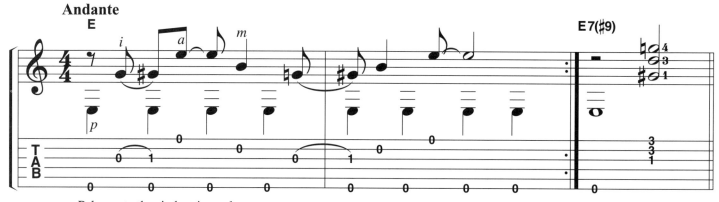

Palm mute the sixth string only.

Glossary

SIGN	TERM	DEFINITION
(arpeggio symbol)	**arpeggio**	The notes of a chord played one after the other, instead of at the same time. (pg. 31, 39, 78)
	chord	Three or more notes played at the same time. (pg. 20)
D.C. al Fine	**_Da Capo al Fine_**	Repeat from the beginning of the piece and end at *Fine*. (pg. 105)
	dampening	Using the left or right hand to stop the strings from sounding. (pg. 60)
(notation symbol)	**hammer-on**	A left-hand finger dropping on a string (like a hammer) to sound a second note. (pg. 66)
	Let ring	Allow the strings to vibrate as long as possible. (pg. 31)
	medley	A song that is made up of two or more melodies. (pg. 13)
	N.C.	No chords are to be played. (pg. 36)
I IV V⁷	**primary chords**	The three chords most often used: I, IV, and V7. See scale degrees. (pg. 71, 86, 89)
(notation symbol)	**pull-off**	Pulling a left-hand finger off a string to sound a second note. (pg. 91)
	riff	A short, melodic group of notes, usually repeated, that has a distinctive sound. (pg. 84)
	ritard.	Gradually becoming slower. (pg. 30)
	simile	Indicates to proceed in a like manner. (pg. 101)
C/D	**slash chord**	A chord in which the lowest pitched note is not the root. C/D is a C chord with a D as the lowest-pitched note. (pg. 9)
	steps	Notes that are one letter name apart, moving in *line-space* or *space-line* order. A half step is the distance of one fret. A whole step is the distance of two frets. (pg. 62)
(rhythm symbol)	**swing rhythm (shuffle)**	Delaying the second half of a beat, creating a long-short rhythm. (pg. 80)

Chords Used in this Book

- These chords are arranged in alphabetical order, making it easy to find a desired chord quickly.

- Left-hand fingerings were chosen for ease of playing, and voicings were chosen for their pleasing sound.

- Students are encouraged to learn as many chords as possible. *Everybody's Basic Guitar Chords* (G1024) contains over 150 commonly used chords.

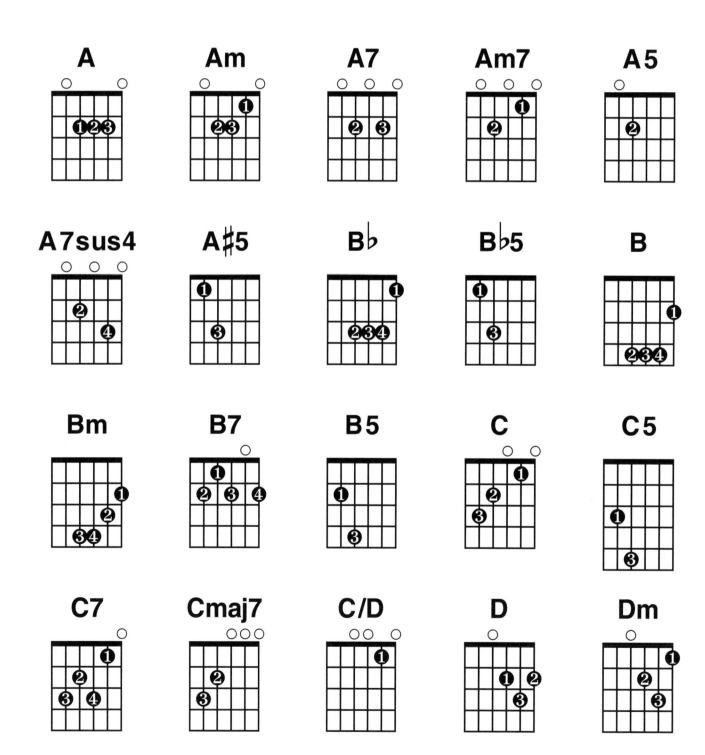

D7

Dmaj7

Dm7
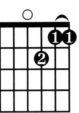

D5
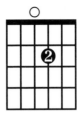

E♭5
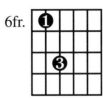

E
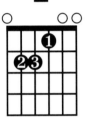

Em
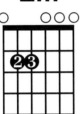

E7
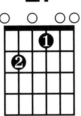

Em7-5
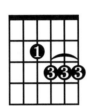

E5
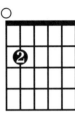

E7(♯9)
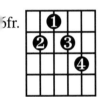

F
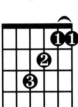

Fmaj7
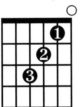

F5
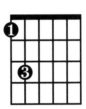

F6
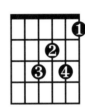

F♯5
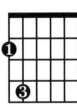

G
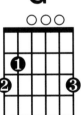

G7
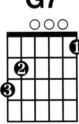

Gm7
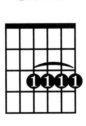

G5
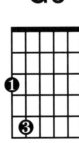

G/B
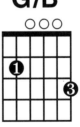

G♯5
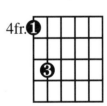

Common Guitar Chords

• This page contains chords that are commonly used by guitarists.